Grandma's Favorite COUNTRY RECIPES

Compiled by Michael J. Liddy and a Lot of Grandkids
Illustrated by Debbie Bell Jarratt

ISBN 13: 978-1-58581-008-6
ISBN 10: 1-58581-008-8

Printed in the United States of America
1st printing © 2007

Copyright © 2007 Golden West Publishers. All rights reserved. This book or any portion thereof, may not be reproduced in any form, except for review purposes, without the written permission of the publisher.

Information in this book is deemed to be authentic and accurate by authors and publisher. However, they disclaim any liability incurred in connection with the use of information appearing in this book.

Interior Book Design: The Printed Page

Golden West Publishers
4113 N. Longview Avenue
Phoenix, AZ 85014
(800) 658-5830
(602) 265-4392

For free sample recipes from every Golden West cookbook, visit:
www.goldenwestpublishers.com

Contents

Breakfasts 9

Salads 29

Soups 41

Breads & Muffins. 51

Appetizers 75

Main Courses 85

Vegetables & Sides 121

Desserts 135

Beverages 149

Index. 157

Preface 7

Breakfasts 10

Traditional Cheese Grits 11	Rice Pancakes – Yes, I Said Rice! 21
Chatanooga Corn Fritters 12	Zucchini Pancakes 21
Rich Man Poor Man Crepes 13	Angel Or Devil Breakfast Casserole 22
Mean Egg and Cheese Bake 14	Popovers 23
Classic (and Classy) French Toast 15	Southern Cornpone 24
Stuffed French Toast 16	Quiche 25
Old Fashioned Pancakes 17	Sunday Quiche 26
Farmland Pancakes 18	Spinach Quiche 27
Perfect Potato Pancakes 19	Homemade Waffles 28
Raised Buckwheat Pancakes 20	

Salads 30

Three Bean Salad 31	Leftover Turkey Salad 36
Bean and Red Cabbage Salad 32	Macaroni Salad 37
Cabbage Slaw 32	Pea Lettuce-Onion Salad 37
Carrot Salad 33	German Potato Salad 38
Chicken Salad 33	Hot German Potato Salad 39
Fruit Glaze Dressing 34	Original Dill Potato Salad 39
Fruit Salad Deluxe 35	Super-Orange-Apricot-Jell-O Salad 40
Sicilian Green Bean Salad 36	Tuna Salad 40

Soups 42

Fresh Tomato Soup 43	Potato Bisque Soup 47
Corn Chowder 44	Pumpkin Soup 48
Potato and Leek Soup 44	Zucchini Soup 48
Cream of Wild Rice Soup 45	Hobo Soup 49
Nana's Chicken and Meatball Soup 46	Yellow Squash Soup 50
Pea Soup 47	

Breads/Muffins 52

Aunt Amy's Apple Muffins 53	Cherry-Pecan Bread 59
Aunt Amy Earhart's Banana Nut Bread . . 54	Chocolate Cinnamon Muffins 60
Aunt Kate's Blueberry Muffins 55	Crusty Biscuits 61
Banana Sticky Buns 56	Date-Nut Pumpkin Bread 62
Beer Bread 56	Dilly Bread 63
Buttermilk Biscuits 57	Gingerbread 64
Old Fashioned Biscuits 57	Gingerbread Cupcakes 65
Bran Muffins 58	Johnny Cake 66
Buttermilk Donuts 59	Herb Sour Cream Bread 67

4   Grandma's Favorite Country Recipes

Hush Puppies 68	Quick Raisin Bread 72
Prune Bread. 69	Sassy Cinnamon Pecan Muffins . . . 73
Pear Bread 70	Squash Muffins 73
Pumpkin Bread 70	Texas Cornbread 74
Pumpkin Muffins—I 71	Zucchini Nut Bread. 74
Pumpkin Muffins—II 72	

Appetizers 76

Hot Artichoke Dip 77	Krazy Meatballs 81
Bacon Roll-Ups 78	Stuffed Mushrooms. 81
Bourbon Hot Dogs 78	Sweet and Sour Meatballs—I 82
Chicken Liver Paté 79	Sweet and Sour Meatballs—II 83
Deviled Eggs 80	Cheese Ball 83
Dilly Dip. 80	Tex-Mex Dip 84

Main Dishes 86

Barbequed Beef 87	"Walk The Flank" Steak 105
Barbequed Chicken 88	"The Other White Meat" Loaf 106
Barbequed Spare Ribs 89	Glorified Hash 106
Beef-Bean-Herb Casserole 90	Mama's Lasagna. 107
Old Time Beef Stew 91	Vegetable Lasagna 108
Oven Beef Stew 92	America's Meat Loaf with Cheese Stuffing 109
Savory Beef Stew 93	Meat Loaf 110
Chicken Breasts In Parmesan Cream 93	Apple Meat Loaf 110
Nana's Nuked Chicken and Dumplings 94	Uptown Manhattan Meat Loaf . . . 111
Beef Stroganoff 95	Mel's Diner Pork Chop Casserole 112
Stuffed Chicken Breasts 96	Savory Pork Chops 112
Southern Mother's Chicken Fried Steak 97	Stuffed Pork Chops 113
Herb Roasted Chicken 98	Stuffed Pork Tenderloin. 114
Chicken and Lima Bean Stew 99	Pork Chop Dinner. 115
Classic Chicken Noodle Dish . . . 100	New England Pot Roast. 115
Chicken Paprikash 100	Pot Roast with Dumplings. 116
Chicken Pie with Crust 101	Pot Roast with Golden Potatoes. 117
Elegant Chicken Pilaf Soup 102	Shepherd's Pie 118
Elegant Pilaf 102	Stuffed Cabbage Rolls 118
"Before There Were Crockpots" Chicken and Rice . 103	Easy Burgundy Stew 119
"Grandma Has A Sore Back" Chicken-N-Rice . . . 103	Simple Sweet and Sour Pork 120
Fried Chicken in Sour Cream-Sherry Sauce . . . 104	Tequila Chicken 120
Ham Steak Shuffle. 105	

Vegetables and Sides ... 122

Baked Asparagus	123	Noodle and Cheese Kugel	131
Traditional Baked Beans	124	Noodle Pudding	132
Boston Baked Beans	125	Easy Potatoes Au Gratin	133
California Baked Beans	125	Shrimp-Stuffed Acorn Squash	133
Beer Batter Fried Veggies 'n' Things	126	Baked Hominy	134
Carrots Vichy	127	Sausage-Zucchini Boats	134
Corn Pudding	127	Spinach Pie	135
Country Hominy Grits	128	Spinach Parmesan	136
Never Fail Dumplings	128	Succotash	136
Green Bean Casserole	129	Sweet Potato Casserole	137
Giblet Bread Stuffing	130	Easy Wild Rice-Mushroom Stuffing	138
Hush Puppies	131		

Desserts ... 140

Amazin' Raisin Cake	141	Grandma's Chocolate Chip Cookies	145
Nana's Fudge Cake	142	The "Best" Oatmeal Cookies	146
Peach Cobbler	142	Peanut Butter Cookies	146
Sunday Special Coffee Cake	143	Apple Pie in a Paper Bag	147
Zucchini Cake	144	Flaky Pie Crust	148
Never Fail Fudge	144	Pumpkin Pie Filling—Fresh	148

Beverages ... 150

Cranberry Punch	151	Peach-Berry Punch	154
Dandelion Wine	151	Root Beer—Home Brewed	155
Gala Holiday Punch	152	Sangria	155
Holiday Punch	152	Orange Slush	156
Hot Apple Cider	153	Wine Cooler Punch	156
Pineapple Lemonade	153		

Index ... 157

Preface

So few words in the English language drum up such emotion and memories as does the term "Grandma." For many folks that word sends us back many years to another time and place despite the fact that the image of "Grandma" is so unique to every one of us. "Grandma" may have been stereotypically plump, German and Midwestern to some, or African-American and Southern to others. And although an image of the loud, boisterous, New York-Italian "Nana" stirring her big vat of tomato sauce may be an easy sell, it's also true that the modern "Grandma" may be fabulous and forty and look more like a picture from *Vogue* magazine than a Norman Rockwell painting.

madre magnifica ~ grote moeder ~ mere grande ~ grandma ~ na na ~ grobartige mutter ~ grande madre ~ mae grande ~ big mama ~

Imagine a posed photograph of all these matronly images, as well as the thousands more we could probably gather from around the USA, and we would have a snapshot of what it is to be purely and simply "American." Which leads me to this book you are holding right now…I mean, what better way to illustrate what "Grandma" means to our cultural psyche than through the only other thing we Americans hold as dear as grandmother…her food!

From freshly made biscuits on a Southern plantation to a Midwest pot roast, the matrons of our families have made their mark in our hearts and in our tummies for generations to come. This collection is both a celebration of, and a big "thank you" to, all the millions of women who, over the years, brought us all together to what we thought was just a great meal. When *really* they knowingly made the great meal just to bring us together.

ML

BREAKFASTS

According to history, after a good night's rest, most people would wake up and "break their fast" with a warm drink (tea or soup) and some form of grain product (rice, oats or bread). Grandma's idea of breakfast was typically formed by her culture coupled with what was already normal fare. Eggs, sausages and pancakes... all staples, when a shift in culinary imagination redirected the course of our nation's most important meal. And so Grandma returned to the cherished recipes of her cultural past by adding doughnuts, potato pancakes, grits, corn muffins and more. Today we are fortunate to have the wherewithal to prepare just about anything our hearts desire, yet we always return to Grandma's favorites.

Breakfasts

Traditional Cheese Grits 11
Chattanooga Corn Fritters 12
Rich Man Poor Man Crepes 13
Mean Egg and Cheese Bake 14
Classic French Toast 15
Stuffed French Toast 16
Old Fashioned Pancakes 17
Farmland Pancakes 18
Perfect Potato Pancakes 19
Raised Buckwheat Pancakes 20
Rice Pancakes 21
Zucchini Pancakes 21
Angel or Devil Breakfast Casserole . . . 22
Popovers 23
Southern Cornpone 24
Quiche 25
Sunday Quiche 26
Spinach Quiche 27
Homemade Waffles 28

Breakfast is serious business in the South and grits are a staple throughout the region. You'd be hard pressed to find a restaurant south of the Mason-Dixon line that DOESN'T serve them. In fact, rumor has it, if a southerner publicly proclaims his distaste for grits, Southern grandmas box them up and send them north to New York City to fend for themselves. It's THAT SERIOUS! Okay…maybe that's a slight embellishment, but in any case, here's Grandma's recipe for Southern lifeblood.

Traditional Cheese Grits

>4 cups **Salted Water**
>1 cup **Quick Cook Grits**
>1/4 cup **Butter** or **Margarine**
>Freshly **Ground Pepper**
>1 cup shredded **Sharp Cheese**

Bring the water to a boil. Add the grits and stir. Cook until thickened (couple of minutes). Add the 1/4 cup butter and freshly ground pepper to taste, stir again and remove from the heat. Add the shredded sharp cheese to the grits and stir.

To create a **Soufflé** from this:

Preheat the oven to 350 degrees while grits cool for 15 minutes.

>3 **Eggs**, separated
>**Cayenne Pepper**
>**Chili Powder**

Beat the egg yolks, add a dash of cayenne pepper, and fold into the grits and cheese. Beat the egg whites until stiff and fold into the batter with a spatula. Bake for 40 to 50 minutes.

Sprinkle with chili powder and serve.

Chatanooga Corn Fritters

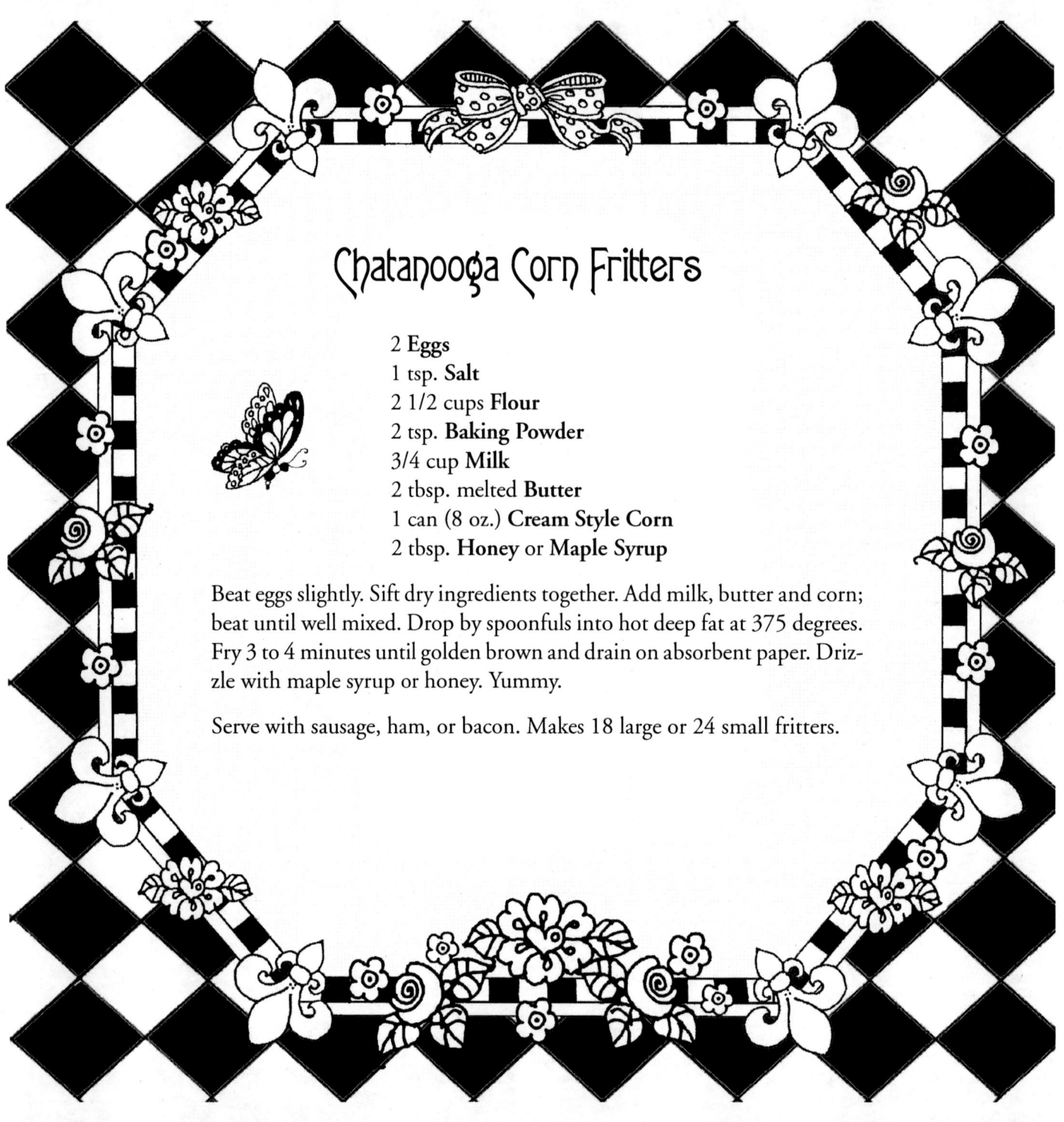

2 **Eggs**
1 tsp. **Salt**
2 1/2 cups **Flour**
2 tsp. **Baking Powder**
3/4 cup **Milk**
2 tbsp. melted **Butter**
1 can (8 oz.) **Cream Style Corn**
2 tbsp. **Honey** or **Maple Syrup**

Beat eggs slightly. Sift dry ingredients together. Add milk, butter and corn; beat until well mixed. Drop by spoonfuls into hot deep fat at 375 degrees. Fry 3 to 4 minutes until golden brown and drain on absorbent paper. Drizzle with maple syrup or honey. Yummy.

Serve with sausage, ham, or bacon. Makes 18 large or 24 small fritters.

Rich Man Poor Man Crepes

1/3 cup **All-Purpose Flour**　　1 **Egg** plus 1 **Egg Yolk**
1 tbsp. **Sugar**　　3/4 cup **Milk**
Salt to taste　　1 tbsp. melted **Butter**

Sift flour, sugar and salt together in a mixing bowl and add remaining ingredients. Mix using an electric mixer. (You can use a thin whisk but you'd better be in shape since you want the batter to be as smooth as silk.) If it's too thin add a little flour; if too thick add a little milk. Refrigerate for a few hours so the batter incorporates and thickens a bit.

Heat a 6-inch skillet on medium heat until a sprinkle of water sizzles on surface. Quickly dry skillet and add a little butter to pan. Crepes are delicate creatures (thus why some cooks are intimidated) so the heat has to be just right. Pour about 2 tablespoons of batter and lift skillet off heat, tilting, so batter covers the bottom of the pan evenly. Return to heat and cook for about 1 or 2 minutes or until underside of crepe is lightly browned. (A heat-resistant rubber spatula is perfect for making crepes.) When bottom is done, flip crepe over onto paper towel and repeat with remaining batter, adding butter for each crepe. Do not turn crepe over in the pan like a pancake. The batter is thin enough that it will be cooked through and any more cooking will just dry it out.

Note: Crepes can be reheated, so take the extras, separated by wax paper, and wrap in plastic wrap. They can also be frozen, but remember to thaw completely.

Crepes have somehow crept up the status scale to the point that many cooks are a little intimidated by them. But not Grandma, folks. She remembers when they were another way to stretch ingredients for those not-so-affluent households of yesteryear, which happened to be…well most of them.

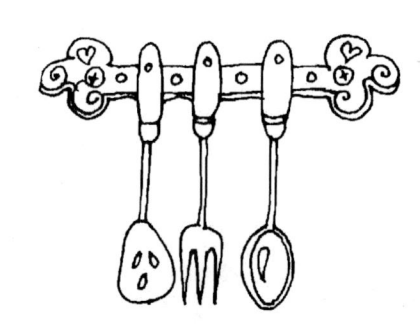

Breakfasts 13

Mean Egg and Cheese Bake

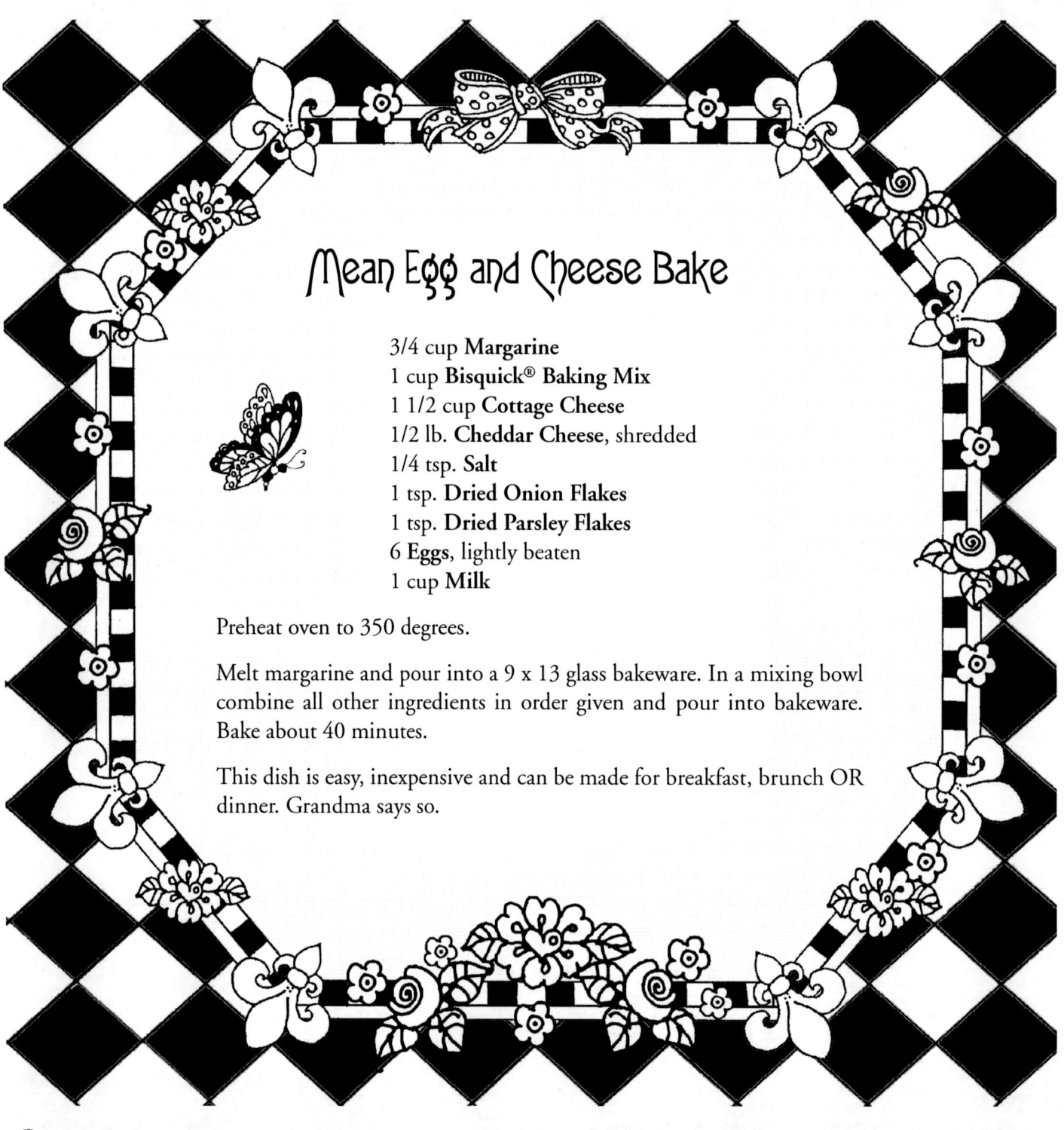

3/4 cup **Margarine**
1 cup **Bisquick® Baking Mix**
1 1/2 cup **Cottage Cheese**
1/2 lb. **Cheddar Cheese**, shredded
1/4 tsp. **Salt**
1 tsp. **Dried Onion Flakes**
1 tsp. **Dried Parsley Flakes**
6 **Eggs**, lightly beaten
1 cup **Milk**

Preheat oven to 350 degrees.

Melt margarine and pour into a 9 x 13 glass bakeware. In a mixing bowl combine all other ingredients in order given and pour into bakeware. Bake about 40 minutes.

This dish is easy, inexpensive and can be made for breakfast, brunch OR dinner. Grandma says so.

Classic (and Classy) French Toast

2 **Eggs**
1/2 cup whole **Milk**
1/2 tsp. **Vanilla Extract**
Pinch of **Salt** and **Nutmeg**
4 slices **Cinnamon-Raisin Bread**
1 1/4 tbsp. **Butter**
1/4 cup **Maple Syrup**

In a shallow bowl, beat together eggs, milk, vanilla, salt and nutmeg. Soak bread in mixture, turning slices until liquid is absorbed.

In large nonstick skillet, heat butter until bubbly. Add bread and cook over medium heat about 5 minutes or until browned; turn slices and brown other side. If any liquid remains pour it evenly over bread as it is cooking.

Serve each slice with syrup.

Like many dishes in our American culture French Toast originated from peasants utilizing any and all ingredients, so nothing went to waste. Stale bread was used specifically for French Toast and actually retains a nice crispness to it without being soggy. Give it a try someday.

Stuffed French Toast

(This is very classy)

1 **Banana**	4 slices **Sourdough Bread**
1 **Egg**	2 tbsp. **Butter**
1/4 cup **Milk**	1/3 cup **Sugar**
1/2 tsp. **Vanilla Extract**	1 tsp. **Cinnamon**
4 tbsp. softened **Cream Cheese**	**Whipped Butter** (optional)
2 tbsp. **Brown Sugar**	**Maple Syrup** (optional)
2 **Strawberries**, sliced	

Remove banana peel. Cut banana in half crosswise. Split each piece lengthwise. Mix egg, milk and vanilla until well blended. Mix softened cream cheese, brown sugar and strawberries together and spread mixture on 1 side each of 2 slices of bread. Place 2 banana pieces on top of spread bread slices and close with other to make sandwiches.

Melt butter in large frying pan over medium low heat. Dip stuffed bread into egg and milk mixture, soaking a few minutes to penetrate into bread. Fry each side of sandwiches to golden brown. (Keep in mind that medium low heat will take some extra time, but it's important that the bread cooks thoroughly enough to warm cream cheese mixture inside sandwich and not burn the outside.) Remove to cutting board.

Mix 1/3 cup sugar and 1 tsp. cinnamon; sprinkle on tops and cut each sandwich in half.

Serve immediately and spread with whipped butter and maple syrup, if desired. Makes 2 each Stuffed French Toast.

Old Fashioned Pancakes

2 **Eggs**, well beaten
2 cups **Milk**
3 tbsp. melted **Shortening** or **Oil**

2 1/2 cups **Flour**
4 tsp. **Baking Powder**
2 tbsp. **Sugar**
1 tsp. **Salt**

Blend the eggs, milk and oil in a large mixing bowl. Sift the flour, baking powder, sugar and salt together. Add the dry ingredients all at once to the blended mixture, but stir only until flour is moistened. Cook on an ungreased nonstick griddle.

Makes about 20 medium pancakes.

Pancakes are another age-old breakfast food that is not just served for breakfast anymore. They taste great any time of the day. Here's a traditional pancake recipe to satisfy the picky pancake purist.

From down on the farm comes a very tasty variation to what we know as pancakes today. But in Grandma's day (okay maybe Great Great Grandma's day) they didn't use the super processed bleached flours we use today. They used ingredients straight from mother earth, which were naturally organic wheat and oats. It doesn't get any more authentic than this.

Farmland Pancakes

1 cup **Rolled Oats**
1 1/8 cups **Milk**
2 tbsp. **Oil**
2 **Eggs**, beaten

1/2 cup **Whole Wheat Flour**
1 tsp. **Baking Powder**
1 tsp. **Salt**
1 tbsp. **Brown Sugar**
Strawberries or **Blueberries** (optional)
Maple Syrup (optional)

Let the oats soak in milk for 5 minutes.

Stir in the oil and eggs; sift the flour, baking powder, salt and sugar into the mixture. Stir just till moist. Pour onto a greased hot griddle and brown on both sides.

For added authenticity, serve with fresh strawberries or blueberries and powdered sugar. Or treat yourself and serve with real, PURE maple syrup. It's more expensive, but, boy, is it worth it.

Perfect Potato Pancakes

2 **Eggs,** separated
1/2 tsp. **Salt**
1 1/2 cups **Milk**
1 1/2 cups sifted **All-Purpose Flour**

1 tbsp. melted **Butter**
2 cups grated **Raw Potatoes**
Fresh chopped **Parsley**
Rendered **Bacon Fat**

Beat egg yolks and blend in salt and milk. Add flour gradually; then melted butter or margarine. Stir in potatoes. Beat egg whites until stiff but not dry; fold into batter. Add chopped parsley and fold once more.

Drop batter by tablespoons on medium-hot griddle greased with bacon fat. (The bacon fat is the key to this delicious, but not necessarily health conscious dish.) Brown on one side, turn and brown on the other.

Option: add some finely chopped onion to the batter and then serve with sour cream or good old-fashioned applesauce.

Raised Buckwheat Pancakes

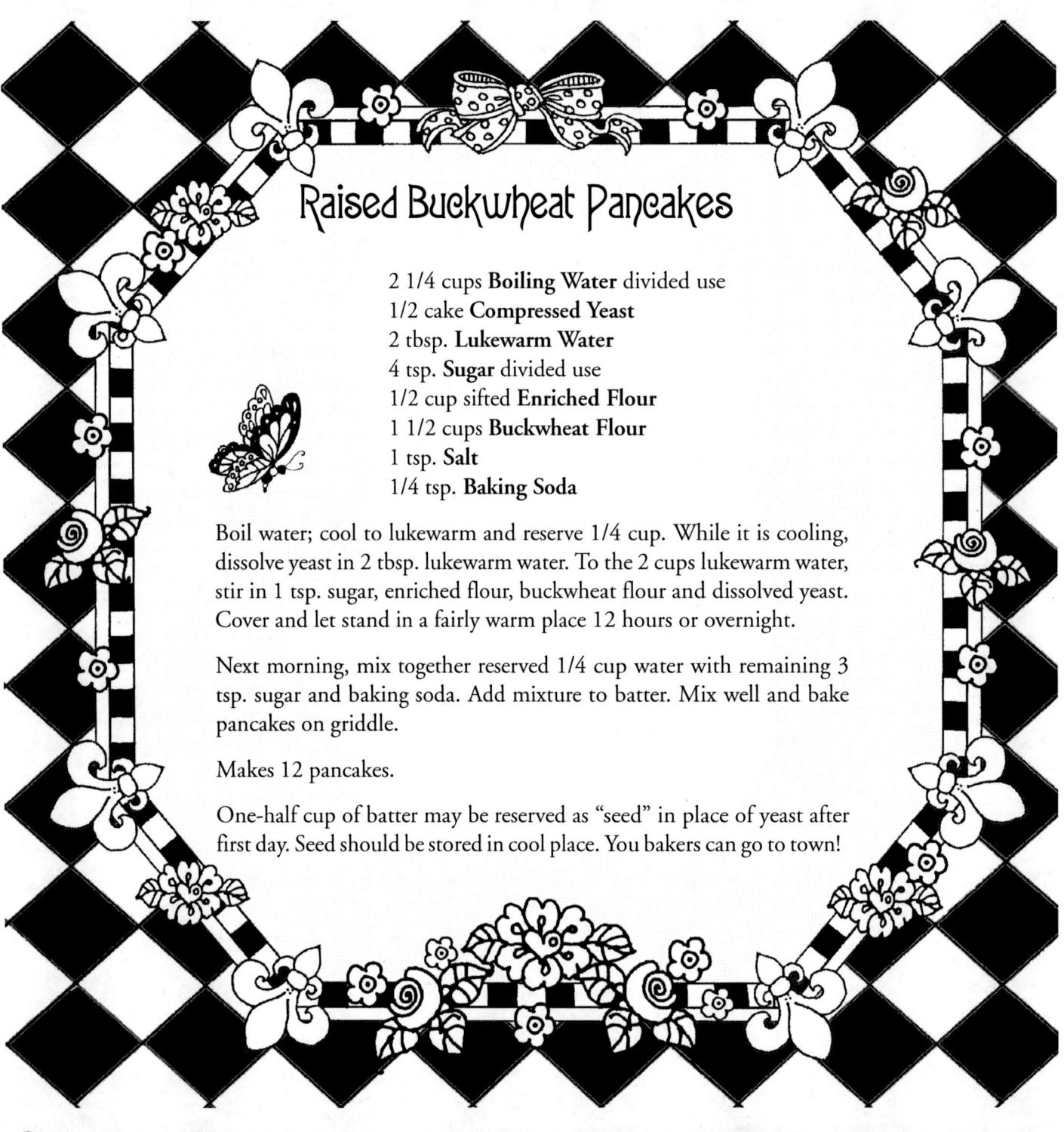

2 1/4 cups **Boiling Water** divided use
1/2 cake **Compressed Yeast**
2 tbsp. **Lukewarm Water**
4 tsp. **Sugar** divided use
1/2 cup sifted **Enriched Flour**
1 1/2 cups **Buckwheat Flour**
1 tsp. **Salt**
1/4 tsp. **Baking Soda**

Boil water; cool to lukewarm and reserve 1/4 cup. While it is cooling, dissolve yeast in 2 tbsp. lukewarm water. To the 2 cups lukewarm water, stir in 1 tsp. sugar, enriched flour, buckwheat flour and dissolved yeast. Cover and let stand in a fairly warm place 12 hours or overnight.

Next morning, mix together reserved 1/4 cup water with remaining 3 tsp. sugar and baking soda. Add mixture to batter. Mix well and bake pancakes on griddle.

Makes 12 pancakes.

One-half cup of batter may be reserved as "seed" in place of yeast after first day. Seed should be stored in cool place. You bakers can go to town!

Rice Pancakes – Yes, I Said Rice!

1/8 tsp. **Salt**
1 cup **Sugar**
1/4 tsp. **Baking Powder**
1 1/2 cups **Flour**

2 **Eggs**
2 cups **Milk**
1/2 tsp. **Vanilla Extract**
2 cups cooked **Instant Rice**

Mix dry ingredients (salt, sugar, baking powder and flour). Whip together the eggs, milk and vanilla and add dry mix to bowl. Add rice (will be slightly runny—don't worry—rice will absorb). Cook on hot greased griddle.

As a variation to the potato pancake we have this recipe for a farm-fresh Italian specialty. They are very tasty on their own, as an accompaniment to eggs, or try them with some tomato sauce and mozzarella for a nice dinner alternative to Eggplant Parmesan. Wow. (Ignore the kids moaning…these are worth the gamble.)

Zucchini Pancakes

2 **Eggs**, well-beaten
3 cups raw, grated **Zucchini**
1 tsp. **Baking Powder**
1/2 cup **Flour** (or a little more)
1/2 cup **Parmesan Cheese**

Salt
Ground Pepper
Fresh **Parsley**
Butter
Oil

Mix together eggs, zucchini, baking powder, flour and cheese. Season with salt, ground pepper and parsley. Fry dollops of batter in a combination of butter and oil. Serve immediately. Grin while eating.

Angel Or Devil Breakfast Casserole

1 box **Croutons**, plain
1 lb. **Breakfast Sausage**, browned
1/2 cup grated **Swiss Cheese**
1/2 cup grated **Sharp Cheddar Cheese**
4 oz. sliced **Mushrooms**
1 tbsp. **Dry Mustard**
1/2 tsp. **White Pepper**, for angel use
1/2 tsp. **Cayenne Pepper**, for devil use
5 **Eggs**, beaten
1 1/4 cup **Milk**
3/4 cup **Half and Half**

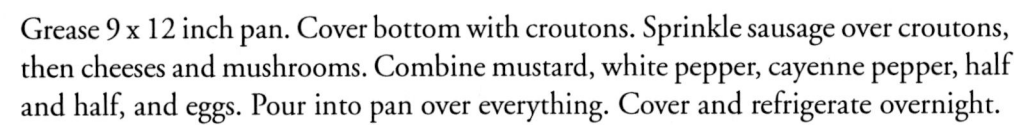

Grease 9 x 12 inch pan. Cover bottom with croutons. Sprinkle sausage over croutons, then cheeses and mushrooms. Combine mustard, white pepper, cayenne pepper, half and half, and eggs. Pour into pan over everything. Cover and refrigerate overnight.

Preheat oven to 350 degrees. Bake for 30 to 35 minutes. Let stand 10 minutes before serving or cover, insulate and off you go.

Serve with a cup of faithful coffee or a Bloody Mary in a traveler's mug.

Now, we're goin' ta church, folks! An absolute classic for your Sunday morning potluck or for the faithful and devoted folk of another breed…sports fans! A phenomenal tailgate dish for that crisp autumn or winter day. It could go either way.

Popovers

3 tbsp. **Butter** or **Margarine**
3 **Eggs**
1 cup **Milk**
1 cup **All Purpose Flour**
1/2 tsp. **Salt**

Preheat oven to 375 degrees.

In small saucepan, melt butter. In large bowl with mixer on low speed, beat eggs until frothy. Beat in milk and butter until well blended. Beat in flour and salt. Spoon batter into twelve 2 1/2 inch muffin pan cups. Bake 50 minutes and then quickly make small slits in top of each popover to let out steam. Bake 10 minutes longer. Serve piping hot.

To make giant Popovers, double the recipe and bake in 8 deep, 7-ounce pottery custard cups. Sit custard cups in jellyroll pan. Bake 1 hour at 375 degrees, then quickly make small slits in top of each popover, bake 10 minutes longer.

Southern Cornpone

2 cups **Corn Meal**
1/2 tsp. **Salt**
1 cup **Boiling Water**

Pour boiling water over the meal to which salt has been added, scalding but not cooking. Stir to consistency of stiff mush. While it is still hot, dip up small portions, shape between palms of hand to form oval shaped pone. Drop in deep, hot grease and fry to a golden brown.

For the true Southerner, cornpone is as regular as having some potato chips with your sandwich. Similar to the hushpuppy, there still remains a debate whether they are or are NOT the same thing. Don't get caught in the middle.

Before we knew quiche by its French label it was known by its English translation —Egg Pie. Here is the simple version of the 1950s "Egg Pie" that grandmas across the land fed their "hard-working" husbands and "well-mannered" grandchildren. (Insert smirk and "ahem" here.)

Quiche

1 lb. **Cheddar Cheese**
1 lb. **Monterey Jack Cheese**
4 **Eggs**
1 cup sliced **Green Olives** with **Pimiento**
1/4 cup chopped fine **Onions**
1/4 cup chopped fine **Green Pepper**

Preheat oven to 350 degrees.

Shred both cheeses. Mix all ingredients well. Butter or spray a 9 x 12 inch oblong cake pan or casserole dish. Pour quiche mixture in pan. Bake 45 to 60 minutes or until lightly brown and bubbly. Let cool for 30 minutes. Very important for it to firm up while cooling. Cut into squares. Serve with some sort of fruit garnish. (Orange slices, grapes, etc.)

To avoid that "Mrs. Cleaver" presentation, replace the olives and pimientos with 1/2 cup sliced green onion and 1/2 cup diced red pepper. You'll get the right colors without the kids running and screaming.

Sunday Quiche

Crust:

> 1 1/4 cups **Flour**
> 1/4 tsp. **Salt**
> 1/4 lb. plus 2 tbsp. **Butter** at room temperature
> 2 to 5 tbsp. **Ice Water**

Preheat oven to 450 degrees.

Mix flour, salt and butter until crumbly. Add ice water and mix until dough is thoroughly moistened. Place on a flat surface and knead into a ball. Place in a plastic bag and refrigerate for several hours. On a lightly floured surface, roll out dough and fit into a quiche dish (11 inch). Bake for 3 to 5 minutes before filling.

Filling:

> 2/3 cup grated **Swiss Cheese**
> 2/3 cup grated **Cheddar Cheese**
> 1/2 lb. cooked **Breakfast Sausage**, ground or chopped links/patties
> 1 cup finely chopped **Ham**
> 1 medium **Onion**, chopped
> 1/2 cup chopped **Green Pepper**, sautéed (optional)
> 8 **Mushrooms**, sliced thin (optional)
> 5 **Eggs**, lightly beaten
> 1/2 pint **Whipping Cream**

Preheat oven to 325 degrees.

After removing crust from oven, layer Swiss and Cheddar cheeses on bottom. Layer the remaining ingredients. Cover with lightly beaten eggs blended with whipping cream. If necessary, add a little milk to cover sufficiently. Bake for about 55 minutes. Serves 6 to 8.

This may be frozen and reheated. It may also be baked first and warmed up in microwave.

Spinach Quiche

1/4 cup grated **Sharp Cheese**
6 tsp. **Flour**
2 tbsp. **Margarine**
1/2 cup **Evaporated Milk**
1/4 cup **Water**
3 tsp. finely chopped **Onion**
1/2 cup canned, sliced and drained **Mushrooms**
1 tsp. **Salt**
Dash of **Pepper**
Dash of **Nutmeg**
2 **Eggs**, beaten
1 package (10 oz.) frozen **Spinach**, cooked, drained

Preheat oven to 400 degrees.

Mix cheese, flour and margarine thoroughly. Press into 8-inch pie pan to form crust. In a saucepan combine milk, water, onion, mushrooms, salt, pepper and nutmeg. Simmer one minute. Remove from heat. Combine eggs and spinach. Gradually add warm milk mixture to eggs. Mix well. (Make sure milk mixture is not too hot or it will cook the eggs.) Pour into pie shell. Bake at 400 degrees for 15 minutes. Lower heat to 325 degrees and bake for 25 minutes.

Breakfasts

Homemade Waffles

2 cups **Flour**
3 tsp. **Baking Powder**
1 tbsp. **Sugar**
1 tsp. **Salt**

2 **Eggs**, separated
1 2/3 cup **Milk**
6 tbsp. melted **Butter**

Mix and sift dry ingredients. Add egg yolks beaten with milk and melted butter. Mix together. Fold in stiffly beaten egg whites. Preheat waffle iron and bake. The key to "crispy, golden brown on the outside moist and steamy on the inside" waffles is a HOT waffle iron. Preheat. Preheat. Preheat!

Serve with strawberries and whipped cream, sweetened with powdered sugar.

Originating in northern Europe, waffles have withstood the test of time, but these days remain primarily in the freezer section of your local grocery store. If you have that old waffle iron in storage next to the fondue pot, do yourself a favor and pull it out sometime. Fresh waffles are a lost art and you realize how inadequate those frozen types really are compared to homemade.

SALADS

A salad is defined as a mix of different foods that are bound by a dressing and they can be served as an appetizer, a second course, or as the main dish itself. In other words, salads can be made up of practically anything you want. Talk about carte blanche! It's no wonder chefs are taking salads to vast new levels. There does remain, however, a soft spot for the traditional notion of salad like Grandma used to make for all our home-cooked meals. Here are some classics we grew up with and still have a hard time passing them by.

Salads

Three Bean Salad 31
Bean and Red Cabbage Salad 32
Cabbage Slaw 32
Carrot Salad. 33
Chicken Salad 33
Fruit Glaze Dressing. 34
Fruit Salad Deluxe. 35
Leftover Turkey Salad 36
Sicilian Green Bean Salad 36
Macaroni Salad 37
Pea Lettuce-Onion Salad 37
German Potato Salad 38
Hot German Potato Salad 39
Original Dill Potato Salad 39
Super-Orange-Apricot-Jell-O® Salad . . . 40
Tuna Salad 40

Three Bean Salad

1/3 cup **Vinegar**
1/3 cup **Salad Oil**
3/4 cup **Sugar**
1 tsp. **Salt**
1/4 tsp. **Pepper** (can be omitted)
1 can (14.5 oz.) **Green Beans**, drained
1 can (14.5 oz.) **Northern Beans**, drained
1 can (14.5 oz.) **Kidney Beans**, drained and rinsed
1/2 **Green Pepper**, chopped
1 bunch small **Green Onions**, chopped

Mix the vinegar, oil, sugar, salt and pepper. Toss with vegetables and refrigerate overnight. Drain and serve.

As kids we ran and hid from this colorful delight because it consisted of that weird textured thing called beans. Even the bravest of the gang only dabbled in the sweet maple covered version, solely because it was paired with a hotdog, which made it palatable. Well, at last, thanks to the enormous popularity of health based diets, beans are finally getting their day in the sun. The positive effects of beans in the diet are almost as nice as the flavor.

Bean and Red Cabbage Salad

1 can (15 oz.) **Kidney Beans**, drained
3 cups shredded **Cabbage**, red or white
1 cup **White Raisins**, soaked in water and squeezed dry
1/4 cup chopped **Sweet Pickle**
1/4 cup chopped **Green Onion**
1/3 cup **Chili Sauce**
1 cup **Mayonnaise**

Combine all ingredients and chill over night. Before serving add mayonnaise and a bit of salt.

Cabbage Slaw

1 large head of **Cabbage**, shredded
2 medium **Onions**, finely diced
1/4 cup **Sugar**

Sprinkle sugar over cabbage and onion.

Dressing

3/4 cup **Sugar**	3/4 cup **Cooking Oil**
1 cup **Vinegar**	1 1/2 tsp. **Salt**
1 1/2 tsp. **Dry Mustard**	1 1/2 tsp. **Celery Seed**

Combine dressing ingredients and bring to a boil. Yes, it may smell up the house a little, but bear with it. In a large bowl pour dressing over cabbage mixture. Let set for 4 to 6 hours. It will stay crisp for a week.

To add some color just grate a little carrot (1/2 cup) or red cabbage and toss.

Carrot Salad

Juice of 1 **Lemon**
1/2 cup **Sugar**
1/4 tsp. **Salt**

Grated rind of **Lemon**
2 cups finely shredded **Carrots**
3 **Green Onions**, finely sliced

Whisk together lemon juice, sugar, salt and lemon rind. Add carrots and green onion, and toss.

Chicken Salad

3 tbsp. **Lemon Juice**
1 1/2 tsp. **Salt**
1/8 tsp. **Pepper**
1 tsp. **Dry Mustard**
1 cup **Mayonnaise**
3 cups cubed **Chicken**

1 cup **Toasted Almonds**
1 tbsp. minced **Onion**
1 1/2 cups diced **Celery**
1 cup **Green Seedless Grapes**
1/4 cup **Light Cream**

Whisk together the lemon juice, salt, pepper, mustard and mayonnaise. In a large mixing bowl combine chicken, almonds, onion, celery and grapes. Toss with dressing and refrigerate for at least 1 hour. Serve on rolls or on greens for a delicious main course salad.

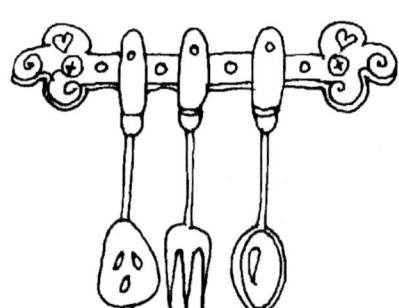

Okay, so you're signed up for that potluck and someone assigns the dreaded "fruit salad" to your name. Oh no! The mess. The discoloring of the fruit. The watermelon boat! AHHHH! What do you do? No problem. You whip together this easy glaze to dress some choice fruits and serve it in a nice bowl with some fresh mint garnish. Less work than Grandma used to do and you get major gourmet status points. But who's counting.

Fruit Glaze Dressing

1/4 cup **Cold Water**
2 tbsp. **Cornstarch**
3/4 cup **Water**
2/3 cup **Light Honey**
3 tbsp. **Lemon Juice** or **Vinegar**
Pinch of **Salt**
Fruit of choice

Use 1/4 cup of cold water to moisten and blend cornstarch.

In small saucepan take 3/4 cup water, add honey and bring to a boil. Stir in cornstarch mixture. Stir constantly until mixture thickens and becomes clear. Remove from heat and add lemon juice or vinegar. Cool thoroughly. Pour over prepared fruit (melons, kiwis, strawberries, grapes etc.) and blend gently until it covers fruit completely.

Remaining mixture may be stored in refrigerator. This is delicious on Apple Salad.

When dealing with delicate fruits like apples and bananas that spoil quickly, toss with some lemon juice to prevent discoloring.

Fruit Salad Deluxe

1 can (11 oz.) **Pineapple Chunks**
1 jar (11 oz.) **Dark Red Cherries**, pitted
2 cans (11 oz. each) **Mandarin Oranges**
2 cans (8 oz. each) **Seedless Grapes**
2 **Apples**, peeled, cored and chopped
2 **Bananas**, peeled
2 cups **Miniature Marshmallows**
1/2 cup **Walnuts**
1/2 cup **Heavy Cream**, whipped
3/4 cup **Sour Cream**
1/4 cup **Salad Dressing**

Drain fruit and combine with marshmallows and walnuts. Fold in whipped cream, sour cream and salad dressing. Chill before serving.

Serves 10.

Sicilian Green Bean Salad

1 can (14.5 oz.) **French-Style Green Beans**
2 stalks **Celery,** chopped
1 can (8 oz.) **Large-Size Peas**
1 **Cucumber,** peeled and chopped
1 **Green Pepper,** chopped
1 **Onion,** diced
4 slices **Sun-Dried Tomatoes,** moistened and chopped

Dressing

1 1/2 cups **Sugar**
1 cup **Vinegar**
1/2 cup **Salad Oil**
2 tbsp. **Water**
Garlic Salt, to taste

Pour over salad and let set overnight.

Leftover Turkey Salad

2 cups chopped leftover **Turkey**
1 cup **Sour Cream**
2 cups **Seedless Green Grapes,** halved
2 tbsp. finely chopped **Parsley**
2 cans (8 oz.) **Mandarin Orange Sections,** drained
2 tbsp. finely minced **Onion**
2 tbsp. **Lemon Juice**
1 cup **Mayonnaise**
Salt and **Pepper**
1/2 cup slivered and toasted **Almonds**

Mix all ingredients together and chill. Top with slivered toasted almonds. Serves 4.

Macaroni Salad

1 cup **Elbow Macaroni**
1/2 cup diced **Cucumber**
1/4 cup diced **Green Pepper**
2 tbsp. **Sweet Pickle Relish**
1 1/2 tsp. grated **Onion**
1/4 cup **Mayonnaise**

1/4 cup **Sour Cream**
2 tbsp. **Milk**
1/2 tsp. **Salt**
Dash of **Pepper**
1 **Egg**, hard-boiled and chopped

Cook macaroni until al dente. Drain, and then rinse with cold water. Place in large bowl. Add cucumber, green pepper, pickle relish, and grated onion; mix well.

In small bowl, combine mayonnaise, sour cream, milk, salt, and pepper; blend well. Pour over macaroni mixture; toss until macaroni is well coated. Gently mix in chopped egg. Refrigerate covered, until well chilled, several hours or overnight.

Makes 4 to 6 servings.

Pea Lettuce-Onion Salad

1 lb. **Bacon**
1 medium head **Iceberg Lettuce**
1 cup chopped **Celery**
1/2 cup chopped **Sweet Onion**

1 box **Frozen Peas**, thawed
2 cups **Mayonnaise**
3/4 cup **Sugar**
Parmesan Cheese, optional

Finely chop uncooked bacon and fry until crisp. Drain on paper towels. Finely chop the head of lettuce and put into a 9 x 13 inch dish. Add celery and sweet onion. Sprinkle peas over all. Prepare dressing of mayonnaise and sugar, spoon over salad. Sprinkle crisp bacon over the top generously and top with fresh parmesan cheese.

German Potato Salad

6 cups peeled, diced medium **Potatoes**
1 cup diced **Celery**
1/2 cup diced **Sour Pickles**
1 medium **Onion**, chopped
12 slices **Bacon**, halved
2 tbsp. **Bacon Drippings**

2 tbsp. **Brown Sugar**
1/2 tsp. **Salt**
1/4 tsp. **Pepper**
2 tbsp. **Vinegar**
2 tbsp. **Water**

Cook potatoes in boiling salted water in a large saucepan 10 minutes, or just until tender; drain, then shake pan gently over low heat to dry potatoes. Stir in celery, pickles, and onion; cover; keep warm. Sauté bacon until crisp in a medium size frying pan; remove and drain on paper towels. Crumble 12 pieces and add to potato mixture; set remaining pieces aside for garnish. Pour off all drippings from frying pan reserving 2 tbsp. in pan. Stir in brown sugar, salt, pepper, vinegar, and water; heat, stirring constantly, to boiling. Pour over potato mixture; toss lightly until dressing is absorbed. Place remaining bacon slices on top. Serve warm.

Hot German Potato Salad

1/2 lb. **Bacon**	1 1/2 tsp. **Salt**
1/4 cup **Bacon Drippings**	1/2 tsp. **Celery Seed**
1/2 cup sliced **Onion**	1/4 tsp. **Pepper**
1/2 cup finely chopped **Celery**	1/2 cup **Water**
3 tbsp. **Sugar**	1/3 cup **Vinegar**
1 tbsp. **Flour**	5 medium **Potatoes**, cooked and cubed

Cook bacon crisp. Drain on absorbent paper and crumble. Sauté onion and celery in the 1/4 cup bacon drippings until tender but not browned. Combine sugar, flour, salt, celery seed and pepper. Stir into onion and celery mixture. Add water and vinegar stirring until smooth. Bring to a boil. Add potatoes and crumbled bacon. Mix thoroughly.

Makes 6 servings.

Original Dill Potato Salad

5 large **Eggs**	1 1/2 tbsp. **Onion Powder**
10 medium **Red Potatoes**	1 tsp. **Black Pepper**
1 large **Dill Pickle**	1 tsp. **Salt**
1 tbsp. **Mustard**	12 tbsp. **Mayonnaise**

Boil eggs. Boil whole, unpeeled potatoes until tender when fork is inserted. Pour off boiling water and run cold water over potatoes until they are cool. Peel the potatoes and eggs; dice potatoes, eggs and pickle. Mix well with remaining ingredients.

May be served warm or cold.

Super-Orange-Apricot-Jell-O Salad

1 can (8 oz.) pitted **Apricot Halves**
1 package (8 oz.) **Orange Jell-O® Mix**
1 can (6 oz.) **Orange Juice Concentrate**

Drain apricots, measure juice and add water to 1/2 cup. Put juice and Jell-O in pan. Bring to a boil and add pinch of salt. Add orange juice concentrate. Puree apricots in blender. Put all ingredients in blender and add 1 cup water. Pour into Jell-O mold or serving bowl after blending. Chill until set.

Tuna Salad

2 cans (6 1/2 oz. each) **Albacore Tuna**
1 tsp. finely diced **Onion**
1 tsp. **Dry Mustard**
6 tsp. **Lemon Juice**
2 tbsp. chopped **Parsley**
1/2 cup **Mayonnaise**
Salt and **Pepper** to taste

Drain tuna and mush with fork. Combine remaining ingredients with tuna in a mixing bowl and chill.

SOUPS

Soup is one of those genres of food that begs the question, "Was soup an invention or was it always here?" The process of boiling water with ingredients in it goes as far back as recorded history and perhaps even further. The word "soup" itself comes from an English term "sop," meaning a piece of bread soaked in liquid, and so long as there was a vessel available, soup was made. With the amazing availability of numerous ingredients today, soup is reaching new heights in originality, but the classics remain. Here are several of Grandma's favorites that nursed us and warmed us until we were all better.

Soups

Fresh Tomato Soup	43
Corn Chowder	44
Potato and Leek Soup	44
Cream Of Wild Rice	45
Nana's Chicken & Meatball Soup	46
Pea Soup	47
Potato Basque Soup	47
Potato and Leek Soup	44
Pumpkin Soup	48
Zucchini Soup	48
Hobo Soup	49
Yellow Squash Soup	50

Fresh Tomato Soup

4 lbs. fresh, **Ripe Tomatoes**	2 tbsp. **Flour**
3 tbsp. **Oil**, preferably **Olive Oil**	6 sprigs **Parsley**
2 cups chopped **Onions**	1 stalk **Celery** with leaves intact
1 cup chopped **Leeks**	8 cups **Chicken Broth**
1 cup sliced **Carrots**	**Salt** and freshly **Ground Pepper**
1 clove **Garlic**, chopped	**Plain Croutons**
1/2 tsp. **Sugar**	

Peel, seed, and roughly chop the tomatoes. You should have approximately 6 cups. In a large saucepan, heat the oil and sauté the onions and leeks until wilted and golden. Add 2 cups of the tomatoes, carrots, garlic and sugar to onions and leeks. Cook it all together, stirring, until the moisture has evaporated and the mixture is thick (anywhere from 10 to 25 minutes). Whisk in the flour and cook for 2 to 3 minutes, stirring, until smooth. Tie the parsley and the celery stalk together, and add it to the saucepan. Add remaining tomatoes, and three cups of the broth.

Cook for 10 to 15 minutes, and thicken slightly. Add the rest of the broth and simmer for 20 minutes. Remove the parsley and celery packet from the soup. Season with salt and pepper to taste.

Serve with croutons.

Soup can be put through a food mill or food processor; however, it tastes just fine if you eat it straight from the pan!

Corn Chowder

Fat Salt Pork
1 **Onion** sliced
4 **Potatoes**, diced
1 quart **Milk**

1 can (15.5oz.) **Whole Kernel Corn**, drained
Salt
Pepper
8 **Crackers**

Cut pork into small pieces (1 inch by 3 inches) and sauté in a pan over a medium low heat. Add the sliced onion and cook 5 minutes taking care not to burn. Strain the fat into a saucepan. Add potatoes and boiling water to fat and cook until potatoes are soft. Then add milk and corn. Heat to boiling point. Season with salt and pepper.

Moisten crackers in cold milk. Serve crackers on top of chowder.

Potato and Leek Soup

4 medium **Potatoes**
5 **Leeks**
2 **Carrots** (optional)
2 quarts **Boiling Water**, more if carrots are used
Salt to taste
3 tbsp. **Sweet Butter**

Peel potatoes, quarter and slice thinly. Remove the tough green parts of the leeks; open to clean away any grit and slice thinly. If used, peel carrots and slice thinly. Add potatoes, leeks and carrots to the boiling water. Cook covered, at a slow boil until the vegetables (particularly potatoes and carrots) are cooked completely and can be crushed with a wooden spoon. Remove the soup from the heat; stir in butter. Use a rice potato masher to crush up the vegetables. This will help thicken the soup.

Serve hot.

Cream of Wild Rice Soup

1/4 cup **Wild Rice** (1 cup when cooked)
1 cup **Water**
1/4 tsp. **Salt**
1/4 cup **Butter** (1/2 stick)
1/2 large **Onion**, diced
1/4 **Green Pepper**, diced
3/4 rib **Celery**, diced
4 to 5 **Fresh Mushrooms**, thinly sliced
1/2 cup **Flour**
4 cups **Chicken Broth**
Salt and **Pepper** to taste
1/2 cup **Half & Half**
2 tbsp. **Sherry**

Place 1/4 cup wild rice, 1 cup water, 1/4 tsp. salt in small, heavy saucepan. Bring to boil and simmer 45 to 60 minutes until rice has puffed and is tender. Add more water if necessary, watch carefully, do not allow too much evaporation. When rice is tender, drain off any excess liquid.

In deep iron skillet sauté onion, green pepper, celery and mushrooms in butter until vegetables soften, about 5 minutes. Sprinkle in flour, stirring and cooking until flour is mixed in. Brown the roux for several minutes while stirring, as this will remove the floury taste.

Slowly add chicken broth, stirring with whisk until well blended. Add rice and season to taste with salt and pepper. Heat thoroughly, stir in cream. Add sherry.

Thickeners for soups can be either flour or cornstarch. It is a good idea to add the thickener with the pan off the heat to avoid the danger of lumping. Flour is good for soups to be served hot. Cornstarch is better for cold soup.

For soups that are too salty, add a raw potato and discard after cooking. The potato will absorb the salt to save the dish.

Nana's Chicken and Meatball Soup

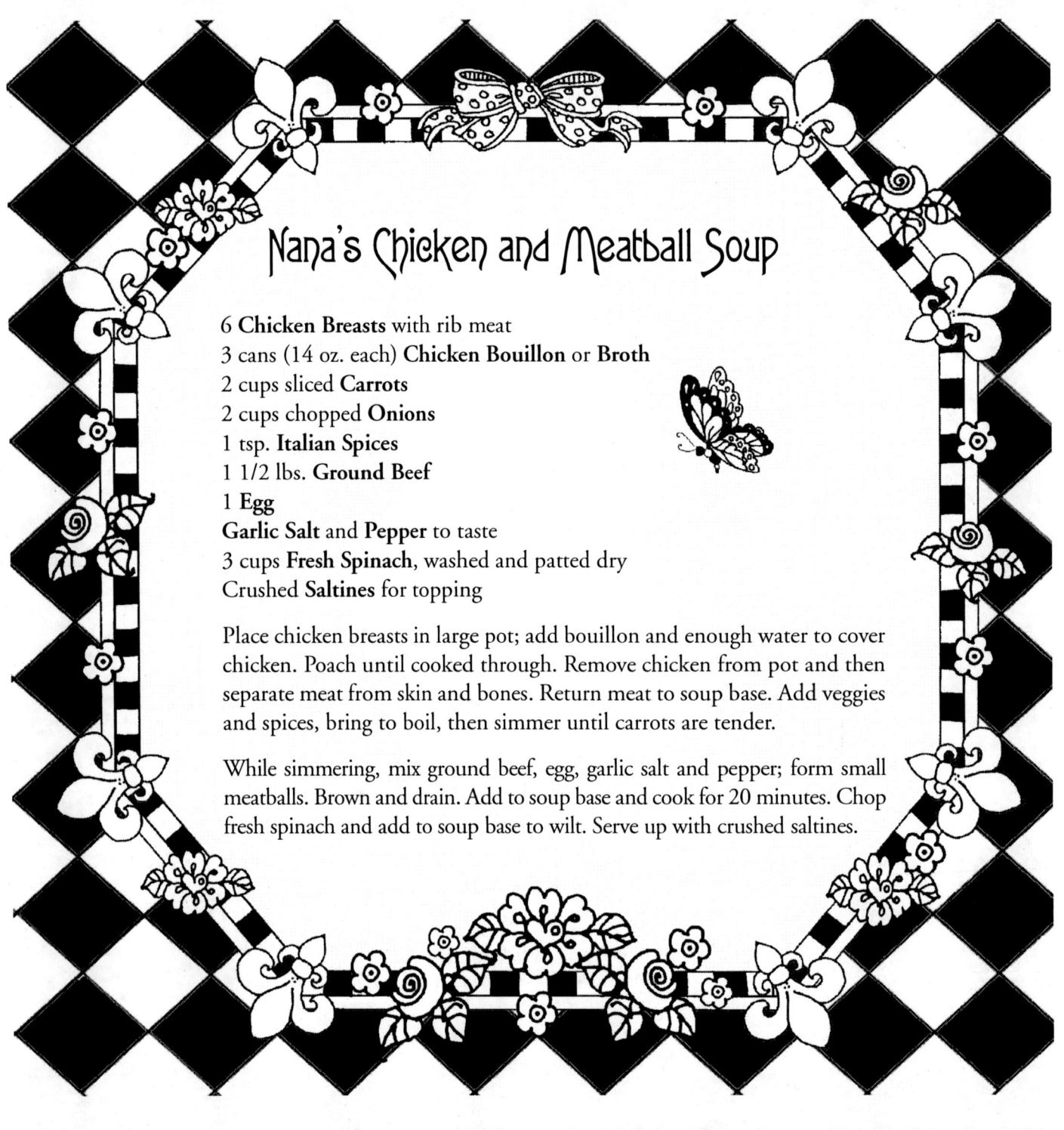

6 **Chicken Breasts** with rib meat
3 cans (14 oz. each) **Chicken Bouillon** or **Broth**
2 cups sliced **Carrots**
2 cups chopped **Onions**
1 tsp. **Italian Spices**
1 1/2 lbs. **Ground Beef**
1 **Egg**
Garlic Salt and **Pepper** to taste
3 cups **Fresh Spinach**, washed and patted dry
Crushed **Saltines** for topping

Place chicken breasts in large pot; add bouillon and enough water to cover chicken. Poach until cooked through. Remove chicken from pot and then separate meat from skin and bones. Return meat to soup base. Add veggies and spices, bring to boil, then simmer until carrots are tender.

While simmering, mix ground beef, egg, garlic salt and pepper; form small meatballs. Brown and drain. Add to soup base and cook for 20 minutes. Chop fresh spinach and add to soup base to wilt. Serve up with crushed saltines.

Pea Soup

1 **Ham Bone** with meat and fat left on
12 cups **Water**
3 **Onions**, chopped
1 lb. **Dried Split Peas** (soaked overnight)
1 **Carrot**, grated
Salt and **Pepper** to taste

Cover bone with water in large pot. Simmer 1 hour. Add remaining ingredients. Cover and simmer 3 to 4 hours.

Potato Bisque Soup

1 lb. **Italian Sausage**, sliced
1/2 cup chopped **Onions**
1 can (28 oz.) **Whole Peeled Tomatoes**
1/4 cup chopped **Parsley**
2 tbsp. chopped **Celery Leaves**
2 **Beef Bouillon Cubes**
1 **Bay Leaf**
1/2 tsp. **Dried Thyme Leaves**
6 cups peeled and diced **Potatoes**
1 cup sliced **Celery**
1 1/2 cups **Water**
1 tbsp. **Lemon Juice**
2 tsp. **Salt**
1/4 tsp. **Black Pepper**

In large saucepan or kettle, brown sausage over medium heat. Add onion and cook 5 minutes. Add remaining ingredients. Bring to a boil, reduce heat and simmer uncovered for 40 minutes, or until potatoes are tender.

Pumpkin Soup

1 tbsp. **Butter**
1 stalk **Celery**, chopped
1/8 tsp. **Thyme**
Salt and **Pepper**
6 cups **Water**

2 **Onions**, sliced
1 lb. **Peeled Pumpkin**
2 tbsp. **Split Peas**
1 tsp. **Parsley Flakes**
1 cup diced **Leftover Meat** (chicken, beef or pork)

Fry onion slices in butter, until golden brown. Add all ingredients to the water except meat. Simmer for 1 hour and blend in blender. Return to pan, add meat and simmer for 15 to 20 minutes.

Serves 6.

Zucchini Soup

1 tbsp. **Butter**
1 tsp. **Olive Oil**
8 small **Zucchini**, diced
1/2 tsp. **Salt**
1/2 tsp. **Pepper**

1 quart **Water**
4 **Eggs**, lightly beaten
4 tbsp. grated **Parmesan Cheese**
1 tsp. chopped **Parsley**
1/2 tsp. **Sweet Basil**

Melt butter in soup pan; add oil, zucchini, salt, pepper and brown lightly. Add water, cover pan and cook for 20 minutes on medium heat. Beat eggs lightly in mixing bowl and add cheese, parsley, and basil; blend together well. Remove from heat; add egg mixture, stirring well. Let stand 3 minutes before serving.

Hobo Soup

A **Meaty Bone**, or **bones** (Beef, chicken, lamb, veal, etc.)
2 quarts **Cold Water**
1 1/2 cups dried small **White Beans**
1 1/2 tsp. **Salt**, or **Garlic Salt**
1/4 tsp. **White Pepper**
1/2 **Bay Leaf**
1/4 tsp. Dried **Thyme**
1/4 tsp. Dried **Marjoram**
1 cup chopped **Onion**
1 cup chopped **Celery**
1 **Carrot**, chopped

In a large soup pot add cold water to a meaty bone. Heat to boiling and after 20 minutes skim surface. Add beans and herbs and seasonings and boil gently for 2 hours or until beans are very tender. Remove bones and trim all meat. Cut meat into bite size pieces and return to pot along with remaining vegetables. Bring to boil and reduce heat to simmer for another 40 minutes. Add salt and pepper to taste.

You can always thin a soup by adding broth, stock, or canned tomatoes.

Yellow Squash Soup

3 tbsp. **Margarine**
1 large **Onion**, chopped
4 medium-sized **Yellow Squash** (about 1 1/3 lbs.) chopped or sliced into thin rings
1 1/3 cups **Water**
1/2 tsp. **Dried Basil**
1 **Chicken** or **Vegetable Bouillon Cube**
1/4 tsp. **Dried Thyme**
Freshly **Ground Pepper**
2/3 cup **Instant Milk Powder**
1/3 cup **Cool Water**
Dry Sherry (optional)
4 tbsp. **Sour Cream**
Fresh or dried chopped **Chives**

In a large saucepan, melt the margarine over medium high heat. Add the chopped onions to the saucepan. Cook until tender, stirring occasionally. Add the yellow squash and continue cooking for two minutes until the squash softens. To the saucepan, add 1 1/3 cups water, the bouillon cube, basil and thyme. Grind pepper in the mixture to taste.

Cover the saucepan, turn heat to low, and simmer the soup base for 15 minutes. Remove saucepan from heat and let the soup base cool to room temperature. Puree the soup base in a blender until velvety smooth.

Return the mixture to the saucepan. In a large cup, mix the milk powder with 1/3 cup cool water until dissolved. Stir the milk mixture into the soup base and cook over medium heat until soup is piping hot. Do not boil.

Ladle the soup into bowls and top each bowl with a dollop of sour cream. Sprinkle chopped chives over the soup and serve immediately.

BREADS / MUFFINS

Bread making is one of the oldest crafts in the world. Loaves of bread and bread making tools have been discovered everywhere from the pyramids to the buried city of Pompeii. Even a millstone for grinding corn was discovered in an archeological site thought to be 7,500 years old. The food was more than likely essential for the creation of civilization, since it required a more community based culture rather than a nomadic one. In other words, like Grandma, bread is the rock of the family. It's no wonder its image is so symbolic. Bread is a staple of life…like Grandma.

Breads/Muffins

Aunt Amy's Apple Muffins . . . 53
Aunt Amy's Banana Sticky Buns . 54
Aunt Kate's Blueberry Muffins . 55
Banana Sticky Buns 56
Beer Bread. 56
Buttermilk Biscuits 57
Old Fashioned Biscuits 57
Bran Muffins 58
Buttermilk Donuts 59
Cherry-Pecan Bread 59
Chocolate Cinnamon Muffins. . 60
Crusty Biscuits 61
Date-Nut Pumpkin Bread. . . . 62
Dilly Bread 63
Gingerbread 64
Gingerbread Cupcakes. 65
Johnny Cake. 66
Herb Sour Cream Bread 67
Hush Puppies 68
Prune Bread 69
Pear Bread 70
Pumpkin Bread 70
Pumpkin Muffins—I 71
Pumpkin Muffins—II 72
Quick Raisin Bread 72
Sassy Cinnamon Pecan Muffins . 73
Squash Muffins 73
Teas Cornbread 74
Zucchini Nut Bread 74

Aunt Amy's Apple Muffins

1 cup **All-Purpose Flour**
1 cup **Whole Wheat Flour**
1/2 cup **Wheat Germ**
1/4 cup **Brown Sugar**
1 tsp. **Baking Powder**
1 tsp. **Baking Soda**
1/4 tsp. **Salt**

1 tsp. **Ground Cinnamon**
1/4 tsp. **Ground Nutmeg**
2 cups peeled, shredded **Apple**
1 tbsp. **Grated Lemon Peel**
2 **Eggs**, beaten
1/4 cup **Skim Milk**
1/4 cup **Vegetable Oil**

Preheat oven to 400 degrees.

In a large bowl, combine all dry ingredients. Stir in apple and lemon peel. In a small bowl, combine eggs, milk, and oil. Add mixture to dry ingredients, stirring just until moistened. Place paper liners in muffin tins. Spoon muffin mixture into tins, filling two-thirds full. Bake for 12 to 15 minutes.

During my college years, my roommate turned out to be a great friend. One reason for the friendship lasting, as it happened, was his return to school after a home visit once a month or so. How I looked forward to those visits home because delicious apple muffins would accompany him upon his return!

Now, as any college student can attest, money is pretty scarce and most meals are eaten in the cafeteria where the phrase "good eats" was as common as snow in the desert. So, on those occasions when the aroma of Aunt Amy's muffins permeated the stale dorm room air, we felt as though we were being offered "a slice of heaven."

Breads/Muffins

Aunt Amy Earhart's Banana Nut Bread

Butter
Flour for dusting
2 cups **Flour**
1 cup **Sugar**
2 tbsp. **Shortening**
4-5 ripe **Bananas,** peeled (the darker the better)
1 **Egg**
1 tbsp. **Milk**
1 tsp. **Baking Powder**
1 tsp. **Baking Soda**
1 cup **Walnuts** (optional)

Butter and flour loaf pan. Preheat oven to 350 degrees. Cream sugar and shortening, add bananas, eggs and milk. Mix dry ingredients together and add to moist ingredients; add walnuts. Cook for first 10 minutes at 350 degrees and 1 hour at 300 degrees.

This banana bread recipe is simple, inexpensive and especially moist.

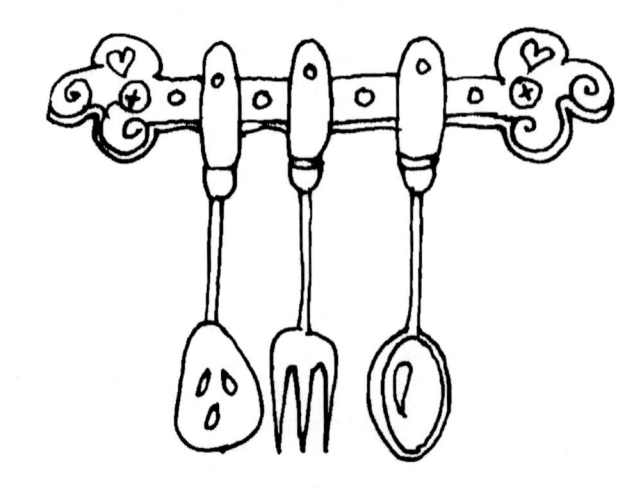

Aunt Kate's Blueberry Muffins

1/2 cup **Butter**
1 1/4 cups **Sugar**
2 **Eggs**
2 cups **Flour**

2 tsp. **Baking Powder**
1/2 tsp. **Salt**
1/2 cup **Milk**
2 1/2 cups **Blueberries**
2 tsp. **Sugar** for sprinkling

Preheat oven to 375 degrees.

Cream together butter and sugar. When very well incorporated, add eggs, beat well. Mix dry ingredients; add 1/4 at a time. Muffins should not be mixed too much; just mix quickly. Add milk alternately. Mash 1/2 cup blueberries, stir in gently by hand. Add rest of whole blueberries by hand.

Place mixture in greased muffin tins 3/4 full. Sprinkle sugar on top. Bake for 25 minutes. Cool slightly before serving.

These are great made ahead and frozen. Fresh whole berries are the best. Makes 1 dozen.

Breads/Muffins

Banana Sticky Buns

1/2 cup packed **Brown Sugar**
1/2 cup soft **Butter** or **Margarine**
36 **Pecan Halves**
2 cups **Bisquick**®

2/3 cup mashed ripe **Bananas**
2 tsp. soft **Butter**
1/4 cup packed **Brown Sugar**

Preheat oven to 450 degrees.

Place 2 teaspoons brown sugar, 2 teaspoons butter and 3 pecan halves in each of 12 muffin cups. Place in oven to melt sugar and butter. Stir Bisquick and banana to soft dough. Gently smooth into ball on a floured cloth-covered board. Knead 5 times.

Roll into rectangle 15 x 9 inch. Spread with 2 tablespoons butter and sprinkle with 1/4 cup brown sugar. Roll up, beginning at long side. Pinch edge of dough to seal. Cut roll into 12 (1 1/4 inch) slices. Place slices, cut side down, in muffin cups. Bake 10 minutes. Immediately invert pan onto serving tray or baking sheet. Let pan remain a minute or two, so butterscotch drizzles down over buns. Serve warm.

Beer Bread

1 can (12 oz.) **Beer,** room temperature
3 cups **Self-Raising Flour**
4 tbsp. **Sugar**
Melted Butter for brushing

Preheat oven 325 degrees.

Mix all ingredients by hand until well blended. Batter will be thin. Grease a loaf pan and dust with corn meal. Bake 1 hour and 10 minutes. The last 10 minutes, brush top with butter.

Buttermilk Biscuits

2 cups **Flour**
1 tbsp. **Sugar**
1 tbsp. **Baking Powder**
3/4 tsp. **Salt**

1/2 tsp. **Soda**
1/3 cup **Shortening**
1 cup **Buttermilk**

Preheat oven to 450 degrees.

Sift dry ingredients together. Cut in shortening. Add buttermilk all at once. Mix lightly. Turn onto floured board and knead lightly. Cut with biscuit cutter. Place on oiled pan. Bake about 15 minutes or until golden.

Old Fashioned Biscuits

3 cups **Flour**
3 tsp. **Cream of Tartar**
1 tsp. **Salt**
1 1/3 cups **Milk**

1 1/2 tsp. **Baking Soda**
1 tsp. **Baking Powder**
1/2 cup **Butter**

Preheat oven to 400 degrees.

Combine all ingredients. Do not roll. Pat out on board; cut. Bake at 400 degrees for about 12 to 15 minutes.

Bran Muffins

2 cups **Boiling Water**
2 cups **All-Bran**®
2 1/2 cups **Sugar**
1 cup plus 3 tbsp. **Shortening**
4 **Eggs**

1 quart **Buttermilk**
4 cups **All-Bran Buds**®
5 cups **Flour**
5 tsp. **Baking Soda**
2 tsp. **Salt**

Preheat oven to 375 degrees.

Pour boiling water over All-Bran and let stand until cool. Cream shortening and sugar, add eggs, then buttermilk. Add cooled bran mixture, All-Bran Buds, and sifted dry ingredients. Keep refrigerated until ready to bake. Fill muffin papers half-full. Bake at 350 degrees-375 degrees for 20 minutes. Makes about 7-dozen.

Raisins may be added to batter. Batter will keep in refrigerator for several weeks.

Buttermilk Donuts

2 cups **Sugar**
3 **Eggs** beaten
1 1/2 cups warm **Mashed Potatoes**
1/3 cup melted **Butter**
1 cup **Buttermilk**

6 cups sifted **Flour**
4 tsp. **Baking Powder**
1 1/2 tsp. **Baking Soda**
1 tsp. **Salt**
1 tsp. **Nutmeg**
Sugar for coating

Add sugar to eggs. Beat until well mixed. Stir in potatoes, butter and buttermilk. Add sifted dry ingredients and mix only until flour is completely moistened. Chill dough 1 hour or longer. Roll 1/2 dough at a time on lightly floured board to 1/2 inch in thickness. Cut with floured butter. Let set 10-15 minutes. Fry in hot, deep fat for 1 1/2 to 2 minutes on each side, turning once. When doughnuts are golden brown, lift from fat and roll in granulated sugar.

Cherry-Pecan Bread

2 cups **All-Purpose Flour**
1/2 tsp. **Salt**
1 tsp. **Baking Soda**
3/4 cup **Sugar**
1/2 cup **Butter**

2 **Eggs**
1 tsp. **Vanilla Extract**
1 cup **Buttermilk**
1 cup chopped **Pecans**
1 jar (10 oz.) **Maraschino Cherries,** drained and chopped

Preheat oven to 350 degrees.

Lightly grease a 9 x 5 x 3 inch loaf pan. Set aside. In mixing bowl thoroughly stir together flour, salt and soda. Set aside. In large mixing bowl, cream together sugar, butter, eggs and vanilla, until light and fluffy. Add flour mixture and buttermilk alternately to creamed mixture. Beat just until blended after each addition. Fold in nuts and cherries. Turn batter into prepared pan. Bake for 60 minutes or until knife inserted in center comes out clean. Remove from pan, cool. If desired, glaze with icing. Can be wrapped in plastic wrap, then foil very securely.

Chocolate Cinnamon Muffins

2 cups **Flour**
4 tsp. **Baking Powder**
1/2 tsp. **Salt**
2 tbsp. **Sugar**
2 **Eggs**, slightly beaten
1/4 cup melted **Butter**
1 cup **Milk**

1/4 cup **Sugar**
1 tbsp. **Cinnamon**
1 tbsp. **Cocoa**

Preheat oven to 425 degrees.

Grease 12 muffin cups, set aside. In a medium bowl combine flour, baking powder, salt and the 2 tbsp. of sugar. In a small bowl, mix eggs, melted butter, and milk. Stir egg mixture into flour mixture. Combine the 1/4 cup of sugar with cinnamon and cocoa. Mix well. Spoon half of the batter into the prepared muffin cups. Sprinkle half of the cinnamon mixture over the batter in cups. Spoon remaining batter on top. Sprinkle with remaining cinnamon mixture. Bake 15 to 20 minutes or until golden brown. Serve hot.

Crusty Biscuits

2 1/4 cups sifted **Flour**
4 tsp. **Baking Powder**
1/2 tsp. **Cream of Tartar**
1/2 tsp. **Salt**
2 tbsp. **Sugar**

1/3 cup **Shortening**
2/3 cup **Milk**
1 **Egg**

Preheat oven to 450 degrees.

Sift together dry ingredients. Cut shortening into mixture to make coarse crumbs. Add milk, then the egg. Mix with fork until dough follows fork around bowl. Knead on floured board five or six times. Roll or pat to 1/2 inch thickness; cut with 2 inch biscuit cutter. Place on ungreased baking sheet about 3/4 inch apart. Bake for 10 to 12 minutes.

Makes 16 biscuits.

These biscuits are great with a hearty stew or pot roast. The crust is perfect for soaking up the gravies.

Date-Nut Pumpkin Bread

1 cup **Butter** or **Margarine**
1 1/2 cups **Sugar**
4 **Eggs**
1 can (16 oz.) **Pumpkin**
1/2 cup **Water**
3 cups **Flour**
1 tbsp. **Cinnamon**
2 tsp. **Baking Powder**
1 tsp. **Salt**
1/2 tsp. **Baking Soda**
1 package (8 oz.) **Dates**, diced
1 cup chopped **Pecans**
1/2 cup **Raisins** (optional)

Preheat oven to 375 degrees.

Cream butter and sugar. Add eggs, one at a time, beating after each addition. Add pumpkin and water. Mix well. Sift together flour, cinnamon, baking powder, salt and soda. Add to pumpkin mixture; beat well. Add dates, pecans and raisins. Mix well. Pour into 2 buttered 9 x 5 inch loaf pans or 2 (1 lb.) coffee cans. Fill 3/4 full. Bake for 60 to 75 minutes, or until bread tests done.

For variety, accent bread with Cheddar Cheese, cream cheese or powdered sugar.

This bread freezes well.

Dilly Bread

1 package **Active Dry Yeast**
1/4 cup **Lukewarm Water**
1 cup **Cream Style Cottage Cheese**
1 tbsp. **Butter**
2 tbsp. **Sugar**

1 tbsp. minced **Onion**
2 tsp. **Dill Seed**
1 tsp. **Salt**
1/4 tsp. **Baking Soda**
1 **Egg**
1 1/2 cup sifted **All Purpose Flour**

Preheat oven to 350 degrees.

Dissolve yeast in water, set aside. Heat cottage cheese in a saucepan to lukewarm. Add butter. Remove from heat. Combine cottage cheese and butter, sugar, onion, dill seed, salt, soda, and egg in a large bowl. Mix well. Stir in dissolved yeast. Slowly add flour, stirring to form soft dough. Place in greased bowl, loosely cover and let rise until double in bulk. Punch dough down. Grease 9 x 5 inch loaf pan. Place dough in pan and grease top. Let rise again until double. Bake 30 to 40 minutes.

This bread is best served with fish, preferably salmon.

To test the rising of yeast dough: the dough is doubled when two fingertips pressed 1/2 inch into it leaves dents that remain. If dents fill in quickly, let rise 15 minutes longer and test again.

Breads/Muffins

Gingerbread

1 cup **Sour Milk** or **Buttermilk**
1 cup **Molasses**
2 1/4 cups sifted **All-Purpose Flour**
2 tsp. **Ground Ginger**
1/2 tsp. **Salt**
1/2 cup melted **Shortening**
1 **Egg**, well beaten
2 tsp. **Baking Soda**

Preheat oven to 350 degrees.

Mix milk and molasses. Sift together flour, soda, ginger and salt into milk and molasses mixture. Combine. Add the shortening and egg and beat until the mixture is smooth and creamy. Place in a greased cake pan and bake for 30 minutes.

Gingerbread cookies and houses are a Christmas classic and thankfully the tradition continues, although the trend now is convenient, ready-to-put-together and ready-made houses. Although the cookies and houses are fun, they do tend to dry out quickly and it's not uncommon to make a quick trip to the dentist after eating a few. My house is a little different. I love the taste of gingerbread and my grandma used to make this genuine gingerbread that just filled the house with the most wonderful aroma, but was moist and yummy and mmm, mmm, mmmmmm!

Gingerbread Cupcakes

1/2 cup **Molasses**
1/2 tsp. **Salt**
1 tbsp. **Ground Ginger**
2/3 cup **Sugar**

2 tbsp. melted **Butter**
1 cup **Sour Milk** or **Buttermilk**
2 1/4 cups **All-Purpose Flour**
1 tsp. **Baking Soda**

Preheat oven to 400 degrees.

Mix molasses, salt, ginger, sugar, butter and sour milk thoroughly by beating. Gradually beat in the flour sifted with the baking soda. Spoon mixture into greased muffin cups. Bake for 20 to 25 minutes.

Johnny Cake

1 scant cup **Cornmeal**
1 tbsp. **Sugar**
1 heaping cup **Flour**
1 tsp. **Cream of Tartar**

1 cup **Milk**
1/2 tsp. **Soda** in 3 tbsp. **Milk**
1 tbsp. **Butter**
Salt

Preheat oven to 425 degrees.

Mix ingredients together. Pour into 9 x 9 inch pan. Bake for 25 to 30 minutes.

Johnny Cake goes by many names, but is more than likely a derivative of "journey cake." Introduced by the Native American Indians and their many uses of corn, it was something that could be eaten out on the trail, as it would keep for many days on a "journey."

Herb Sour Cream Bread

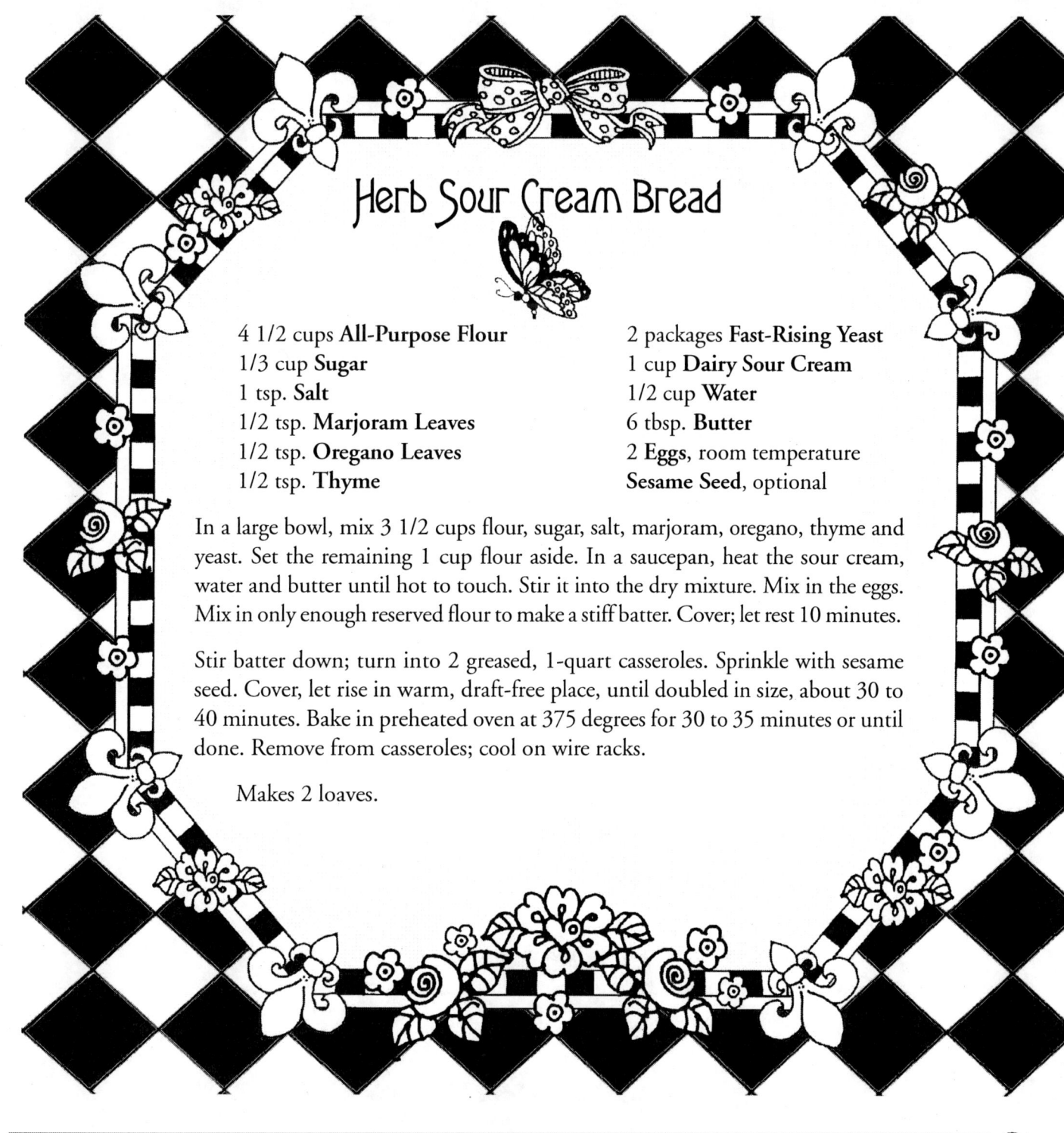

4 1/2 cups **All-Purpose Flour**
1/3 cup **Sugar**
1 tsp. **Salt**
1/2 tsp. **Marjoram Leaves**
1/2 tsp. **Oregano Leaves**
1/2 tsp. **Thyme**

2 packages **Fast-Rising Yeast**
1 cup **Dairy Sour Cream**
1/2 cup **Water**
6 tbsp. **Butter**
2 **Eggs**, room temperature
Sesame Seed, optional

In a large bowl, mix 3 1/2 cups flour, sugar, salt, marjoram, oregano, thyme and yeast. Set the remaining 1 cup flour aside. In a saucepan, heat the sour cream, water and butter until hot to touch. Stir it into the dry mixture. Mix in the eggs. Mix in only enough reserved flour to make a stiff batter. Cover; let rest 10 minutes.

Stir batter down; turn into 2 greased, 1-quart casseroles. Sprinkle with sesame seed. Cover, let rise in warm, draft-free place, until doubled in size, about 30 to 40 minutes. Bake in preheated oven at 375 degrees for 30 to 35 minutes or until done. Remove from casseroles; cool on wire racks.

Makes 2 loaves.

Hush Puppies

1 **Egg**, beaten
1 cup **Buttermilk**
1/2 cup finely chopped **Onion**
1/4 cup **Water**
1 3/4 cup **Cornmeal**
1/2 cup **All-Purpose Flour**

1 tbsp. **Sugar**
2 tbsp. **Baking Powder**
1 tsp. **Salt**
1/2 tsp. **Baking Soda**
Shortening or **Cooking Oil** for deep frying

Blend egg, buttermilk, onion and water, and set aside. Combine cornmeal, flour, sugar, baking powder, salt and soda. Add egg mixture to cornmeal mixture; stir just to moisten. Refrigerate overnight. Drop batter by tablespoons into deep hot (375 F.) fryer. Fry for about 2 minutes or until golden brown, turning once. Drain on paper towels. Serve hot with butter.

Makes about 24.

There are many variations on the origin of "hushpuppies." Confederate soldiers, the very poor in the South who were hiding from the Union Army, used salamander as food and would toss these corn fritters to the dogs to keep them from barking. The salamanders were known as water puppies and would be gathered and placed in batter and fried to eat, but to hide the embarrassing truth—were renamed "hushpuppies."

Hushpuppies, the food, originated in the settlement of Nouvell Orleans (later called New Orleans, Louisiana), shortly after 1727. They were most likely created by a group of Ursuline nuns who had come over from France. The nuns turned cornmeal into a food that they named croquettes de maise. The frugal food spread quickly throughout the south.

Prune Bread

1 3/4 cups **Flour**	1 tsp. **Salt**
3/4 cup **Sugar**	3/4 cup **Milk**
2/3 cup **Wheat Germ**	1/4 cup **Oil**
2/3 cup finely chopped **Pecans**	1 **Egg**
2 tbsp. **Butter** or **Margarine**	2 tbsp. **Orange Peel**
3 tsp. **Baking Powder**	1 cup chopped cooked **Prunes**

Preheat oven to 350 degrees.

Combine 2 tbsp. flour, 3 tbsp. sugar, 2 tbsp. wheat germ and 3 tbsp. pecans in small bowl. Cut in butter until mixture is crumbly. Set aside for topping. Combine remaining flour, sugar, wheat germ and pecans in large bowl. Add baking powder and salt. Stir well to blend. Combine milk, oil, egg and orange peel. Beat slightly. Add milk mixture to dry ingredients all at once. Mix until thoroughly moistened. Stir in prunes. Pour into well-greased 9 x 5 inch loaf pan. Sprinkle reserved topping mixture evenly over batter. Bake for 60 to 70 minutes, or until pick inserted in center comes out clean. Cool on rack 5 minutes before removing from pan. Makes 1 loaf.

Note: Traditionally made with white flour, this bread can be easily transformed into a very healthful loaf by using whole wheat flour.

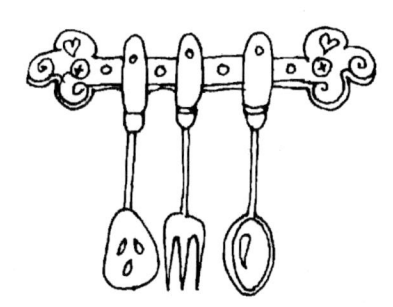

Pear Bread

3 **Eggs**, beaten
2 cups **Sugar**
1 cup **Vegetable Oil**
2 cups chopped **Pears**
2 tsp. **Vanilla Extract**
3 cups sifted **Flour**
1 tsp. **Baking Soda**
1/4 tsp. **Baking Powder**
1 tsp. **Salt**
3 tsp. **Cinnamon**
Chopped **Walnuts** (optional)

Preheat oven to 325 degrees.

In large bowl, beat together eggs, sugar, and oil. Fold in pears and vanilla. In medium bowl, sift flour, baking soda, baking powder, salt and cinnamon. Mix into pear mixture. Pour into two greased pans. Bake 60 minutes.

Pumpkin Bread

2/3 cup **Shortening**
3 cups **Sugar**
4 **Eggs**
2 cups canned **Pumpkin**
2/3 cup **Water**
1 tsp. **Salt**
3 1/3 cups **Flour**
1/2 tsp. **Baking Powder**
2 tsp. **Baking Soda**
1 tsp. **Cinnamon**
1/2 tsp. **Cloves**
3/4 cup chopped **Nuts**

Preheat oven to 350 degrees.

Add ingredients in order given above, starting with the first column. Grease loaf pans. Bake 1 hour and 25 minutes.

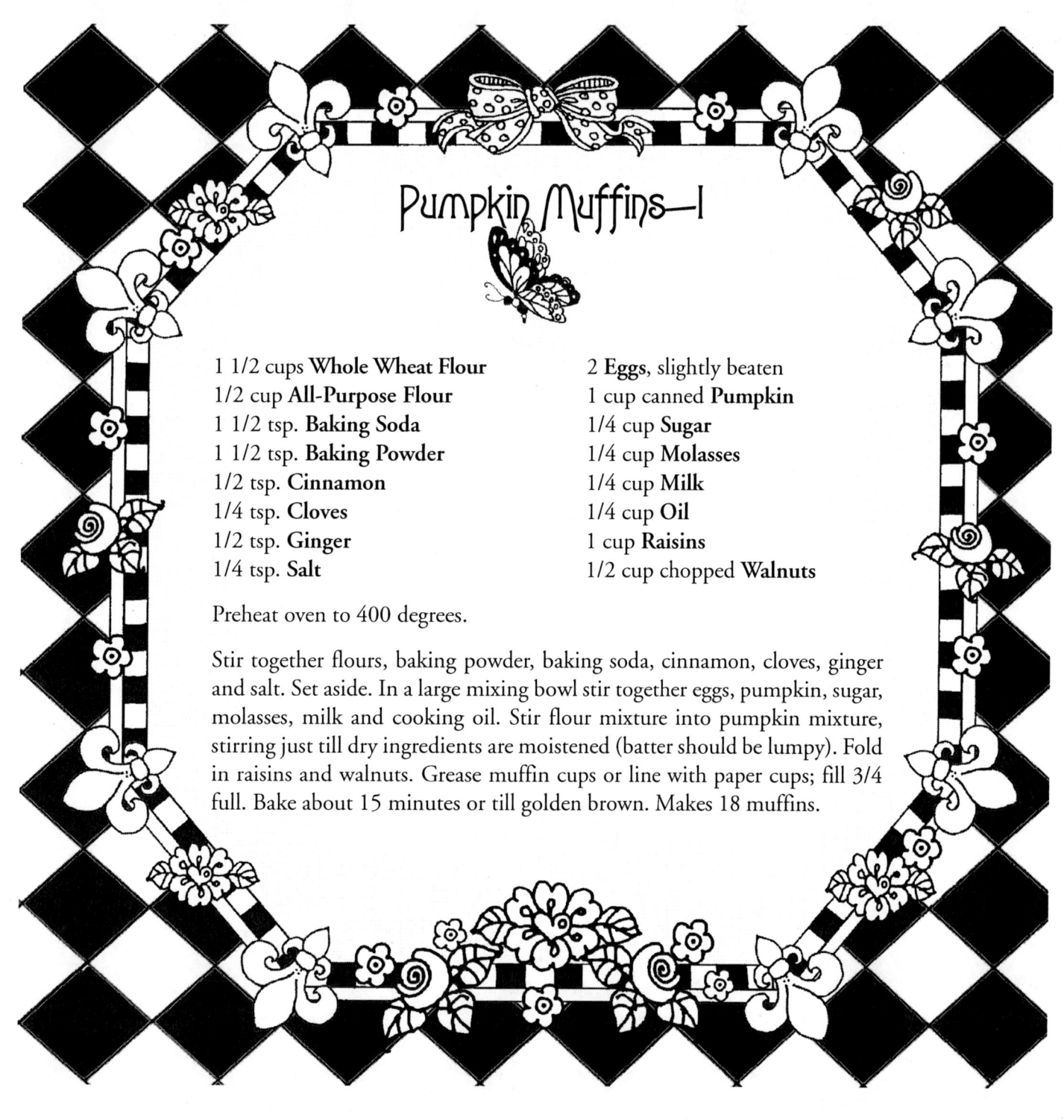

Pumpkin Muffins—I

1 1/2 cups **Whole Wheat Flour**
1/2 cup **All-Purpose Flour**
1 1/2 tsp. **Baking Soda**
1 1/2 tsp. **Baking Powder**
1/2 tsp. **Cinnamon**
1/4 tsp. **Cloves**
1/2 tsp. **Ginger**
1/4 tsp. **Salt**

2 **Eggs**, slightly beaten
1 cup canned **Pumpkin**
1/4 cup **Sugar**
1/4 cup **Molasses**
1/4 cup **Milk**
1/4 cup **Oil**
1 cup **Raisins**
1/2 cup chopped **Walnuts**

Preheat oven to 400 degrees.

Stir together flours, baking powder, baking soda, cinnamon, cloves, ginger and salt. Set aside. In a large mixing bowl stir together eggs, pumpkin, sugar, molasses, milk and cooking oil. Stir flour mixture into pumpkin mixture, stirring just till dry ingredients are moistened (batter should be lumpy). Fold in raisins and walnuts. Grease muffin cups or line with paper cups; fill 3/4 full. Bake about 15 minutes or till golden brown. Makes 18 muffins.

Pumpkin Muffins—II

1 1/3 cup softened **Butter**
1/4 cup **Sugar**
1 **Egg**
2/3 cup mashed **Pumpkin**
1 1/2 cups **All-Purpose Flour**
1 3/4 tsp. **Baking Powder**
1/2 tsp. **Baking Soda**
1/2 tsp. **Salt**
3/4 tsp. **Ground Ginger**
1/2 tsp. **Ground Nutmeg**
1/8 tsp. **Ground Cloves**
1/2 cup **Milk**
1/2 cup **Currants**, optional

Preheat oven to 350 degrees.

Cream butter; gradually add sugar, beating until light and fluffy. Add egg and pumpkin; beat well. Combine next seven ingredients and add to creamed mixture alternating with milk, beginning and ending with flour mixture. Stir in currants. Spoon batter into paper-lined muffin cups, filling 3/4 full. Bake for 20 minutes.

Makes one dozen.

Quick Raisin Bread

2 cups **Raisins**
2 cups **Hot Water**
2 tsp. **Baking Soda**
1/2 cup **Shortening**
2 cups **Brown Sugar**
2 **Eggs**, beaten
1 tsp. **Vanilla Extract**
4 cups **Flour**
1 1/2 tsp. **Salt**
1 cup **Walnuts** (optional)

Preheat oven to 350 degrees.

Bring raisins and water to a boil. Remove from stove. Add baking soda and let cool. Cream shortening and sugar. Add beaten eggs. Add other ingredients alternately with raisins. Bake 1 hour.

Sassy Cinnamon Pecan Muffins

1 1/2 cups **Flour**
1/4 cup **Sugar**
1/4 cup **Brown Sugar**
2 tsp. **Baking Powder**
1/2 tsp. **Salt**

1/2 tsp. **Cinnamon**
1 **Egg**, beaten
1/2 cup **Oil**
1/2 cup **Milk**
1/2 cup chopped **Pecans**

Preheat oven to 400 degrees.

Sift together flour, sugars, baking powder, salt and cinnamon into bowl. Combine egg, oil and milk in another bowl. Mix well. Slowly add to dry ingredients. Stir until just mixed. Fold in pecans. Fill greased muffin cups 2/3 full. Bake for 20 to 25 minutes.

Makes one dozen.

Squash Muffins

1 **Egg**
4 tbsp. **Sugar**
1/2 cup **Milk**
1/2 cup cooked **Squash**

1 3/4 cup **Flour**
1/2 tsp. **Salt**
2 tsp. **Cream of Tartar**
1 tsp. **Baking Soda**
4 tbsp. **Shortening**

Preheat oven to 400 degrees.

Beat egg and sugar, add milk and squash. Add dry ingredients sifted together; then shortening. Bake in greased muffin pan, filled 2/3 full, for 20 to 25 minutes.

Texas Cornbread

1 1/2 cups **Yellow Cornmeal**
1 tsp. **Salt**
1 tbsp. **Baking Powder**
2 **Eggs**, beaten
2 tbsp. chopped **Green Pepper**

1 cup **Sour Cream**
1 cup **Cream-Style Corn**
1/4 cup **Vegetable Oil**
2 **Jalapeño Peppers**, chopped
1 cup grated **Cheddar Cheese**

Preheat oven to 350 degrees.

Combine all the ingredients except cheese. Pour half the batter into a hot, greased 10-inch iron skillet; sprinkle evenly with half the cheese. Repeat layers. Bake for 35 to 40 minutes. Serves 12.

Zucchini Nut Bread

3 cups **Flour**
1 tsp. **Baking Soda**
2 scant cups **Sugar**
1/4 tsp. **Baking Powder**
1 cup **Oil**
1 tsp. **Cinnamon**
2 cups grated, washed and scrubbed **Zucchini**
1/2 cup broken-piece **Walnuts**
3 tsp. **Vanilla Extract**
1/4 cups **Raisins** (optional)
3 **Eggs**

Preheat oven to 350 degrees.

Mix all ingredients together. Pour into 2 greased loaf pans. Bake for 1 hour.

APPETIZERS

Appetizers have a long history, dating back to ancient Rome and even the Greeks, as a great way to stretch out a meal for hours at a time resulting in a gluttonous feast. American history on the other hand, doesn't really offer much in the appetizer world since colonists were not very affluent. "Roughing it" is an understatement considering the birth of a nation and a new culture, as many were mixed and didn't have the luxury of a variety of foods. If anything was served before a main meal in our early days, it was a hearty bowl of Grandma's soup. In fact it wasn't until the 1950s when America really hit an economic stride after WWII that moms and grandmas began their surge of cocktail parties, where the appetizer came to the forefront, showing up on menus everywhere.

Appetizers

Hot Artichoke Dip 77
Bacon Roll-Ups 78
Bourbon Hot Dogs 78
Chicken Liver Paté 79
Deviled Eggs. 80
Dilly Dip 80
Krazy Meatballs 81
Stuffed Mushrooms 81
Sweet and Sour Meatballs—I 82
Sweet and Sour Meatballs—II 82
Cheese Ball 83
Tex-Mex Dip 84

Hot Artichoke Dip

    Cooked fresh **Artichoke Leaves**
    Raw Zucchini Spears
    Whole Mushrooms, sliced (large or small)
    Chunks of **Fresh Bread**

In food processor or blender, purée:

    1 can (13-3/4 oz.) **Artichoke Hearts** in water, drained or
        2 small jars of partially drained **Marinated Artichokes**
    1/2 cup **Sour Cream**
    1/3 cup **Mayonnaise**
    1/4 cup grated **Parmesan Cheese**

Pour into a 2 1/2 to 3 cup ovenproof casserole. Preheat oven to 350 degrees.

In small bowl mix:

    1/4 cup fresh **Bread Crumbs**
    1 tbsp. chopped **Parsley**
    2 tbsp. melted **Butter** or **Margarine**

Sprinkle over artichoke mixture. Bake 25 minutes or until hot.

Makes 2 cups.

Appetizers

Bacon Roll-Ups

1 lb. **Bacon**
1 large package **Cream Cheese**, softened
1 loaf **White Bread,** crusts removed
1 package **Onion Soup Mix**

Preheat oven to 400 degrees.

Combine cheese and soup mix. Spread on bread and cut in fourths. Roll and wrap in 1/2 slice bacon. Fasten with toothpicks. Bake until bacon begins to crisp.

Bourbon Hot Dogs

1 bottle (16 oz.) **Ketchup**
1/2 cup **Bourbon**
1/2 cup **Brown Sugar**
1 lb. **Hot Dogs**

Mix ketchup, bourbon and sugar; set sauce aside. Cut each hot dog into 4 pieces and cut an X in each end. Boil hot dogs for 5 minutes. Hot dog ends will curl out to make flowerets. Marinate in sauce overnight. Heat and serve.

Chicken Liver Paté

This recipe is made for a blender or food processor. If you don't have one, don't try it!

1 medium **Onion,** chopped	1/2 tsp. **Allspice**
1 clove **Garlic,** chopped	1 tbsp. **Salt**
2 **Eggs**	1 tsp. **White Pepper**
1 lb. **Chicken Livers**	1/4 cup **Butter**
1/4 cup **Flour**	1 cup **Heavy Cream**
1/2 tsp. **Ground Ginger**	**Pumpernickel Bread**

Preheat oven to 325 degrees.

Combine onion, garlic and eggs in blender/processor at high speed for one minute. Add livers and blend two minutes longer. Add the next seven ingredients and blend at high speed one or two minutes more, until smooth. Pour into well-greased one quart baking dish and cover. Set in pan of hot water and bake for three hours. Remove cover and cool paté. Replace cover and chill thoroughly, at least 4 hours or overnight. To serve, spread paté on squares of pumpernickel bread.

Deviled Eggs

12 **Eggs**, hard-boiled
1/2 tsp. **Worcestershire Sauce**
1/3 cup **Mayonnaise**
1 tsp. prepared **Mustard**
2 tsp. **Horseradish**
Salt and **Pepper**
Paprika

Cut eggs into halves. Remove yolks, mash and mix with next five ingredients. Force mixture through decorative pastry tube into white halves. In a pinch, just use a clear plastic storage bag and cut a small tip off the corner. Sprinkle with paprika. Serve chilled. Makes 24.

Dilly Dip

1 cup **Sour Cream**
2 tsp. **Herb de Provence**, Spice Island Brand®
1 cup **Mayonnaise**
1 tbsp. chopped dried **Parsley**
2 tsp. **Dill Weed**
2 tsp. minced dried **Onions**
1/2 cup **Plain Yogurt**

Mix all ingredients well. Refrigerate overnight. Good with raw vegetables, crackers, chips or baked potatoes.

Krazy Meatballs

2 lbs. **Ground Beef**
1 cup **Bread Crumbs**
2 **Eggs**, beaten
1 package **Lipton Onion Soup Mix**

1 can (28 oz.) **Sauerkraut**, rinsed once
1 can (16 oz.) **Whole Cranberries** in sauce
1 jar (12 oz.) **Chili Sauce**
1 cup **Brown Sugar**

Preheat oven to 350 degrees.

Mix ground beef, breadcrumbs, eggs, and soup mix. Roll into bite-size meatballs. Place in 9 x 12 pan; set aside. In separate bowl, mix sauerkraut, cranberries, chili sauce and brown sugar. Pour over meatballs. Bake 1 1/2 hours, stirring once after 1 hour and again when done. Serve warm.

Stuffed Mushrooms

1 lb. large **Mushrooms**
1 cup **Bread Crumbs**
3 tbsp. grated **Parmesan Cheese**
1 tbsp. chopped fresh **Parsley**
2 tbsp. melted **Butter**

1 clove **Garlic**, chopped
1 small **Onion**, chopped
Salt and **Pepper** to taste
6 tbsp. **Olive Oil**

Preheat oven 350 degrees.

Clean and remove stems of mushrooms. Chop stems very fine. Mix stem pieces, breadcrumbs, cheese, parsley, butter, garlic, onion and salt and pepper. Fill mushroom caps. Pour 2 tbsp. of olive oil in bottom of baking dish and place mushroom caps in pan stuffed side up. Drizzle remaining olive oil (4 tbsp.) evenly over top of mushrooms. Bake for 20 minutes. Serve VERY hot.

Serves 4 to 6.

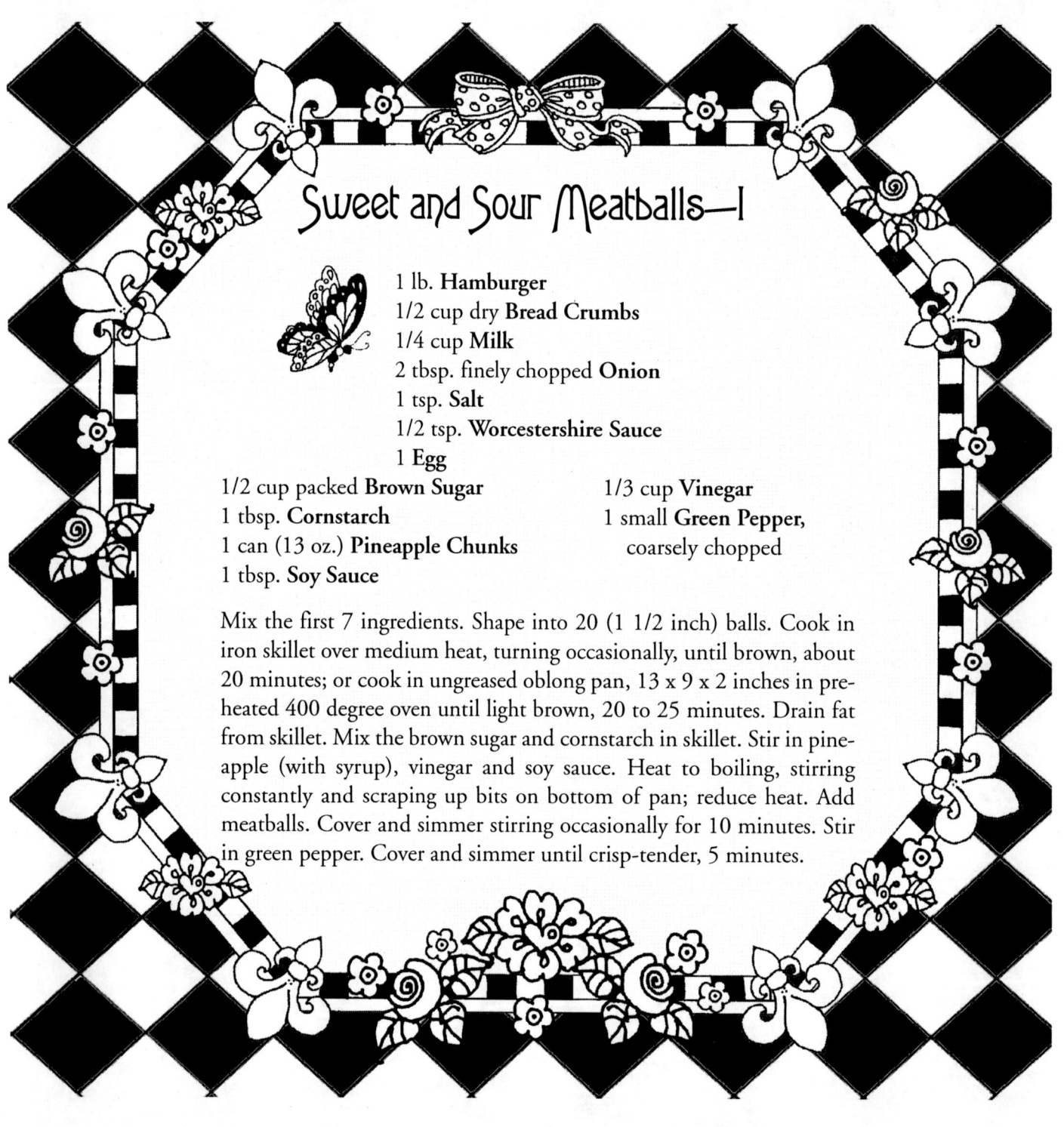

Sweet and Sour Meatballs—1

1 lb. **Hamburger**
1/2 cup dry **Bread Crumbs**
1/4 cup **Milk**
2 tbsp. finely chopped **Onion**
1 tsp. **Salt**
1/2 tsp. **Worcestershire Sauce**
1 **Egg**

1/2 cup packed **Brown Sugar**
1 tbsp. **Cornstarch**
1 can (13 oz.) **Pineapple Chunks**
1 tbsp. **Soy Sauce**
1/3 cup **Vinegar**
1 small **Green Pepper**, coarsely chopped

Mix the first 7 ingredients. Shape into 20 (1 1/2 inch) balls. Cook in iron skillet over medium heat, turning occasionally, until brown, about 20 minutes; or cook in ungreased oblong pan, 13 x 9 x 2 inches in pre-heated 400 degree oven until light brown, 20 to 25 minutes. Drain fat from skillet. Mix the brown sugar and cornstarch in skillet. Stir in pineapple (with syrup), vinegar and soy sauce. Heat to boiling, stirring constantly and scraping up bits on bottom of pan; reduce heat. Add meatballs. Cover and simmer stirring occasionally for 10 minutes. Stir in green pepper. Cover and simmer until crisp-tender, 5 minutes.

Sweet and Sour Meatballs—II

2 lbs. **Ground Beef**
1 raw **Potato**, grated
2 tbsp. **Ketchup**
2 tbsp. **French Dressing**
1/2 tsp. each **Onion** and **Garlic Salt**

Mix ingredients together. Shape into small balls and place on cookie sheet. Brown slightly under broiler, not necessary to turn. Prepare following sauce in a saucepan and bring to a boil.

1 bottle (16 oz.) **Ketchup**
1 jar (12 oz.) **Tomato Preserves**
2 cups **Water**
Juice of 1/2 **Lemon**

Add meatballs and simmer for one hour.

Cheese Ball

2 packages (8 oz. each) **Cream Cheese**
1 **Onion**, finely chopped
1 jar (5 oz.) **Kraft® Old English Cheese Spread**
Dash of **Worcestershire Sauce**
Salt and **Pepper** to taste
1 package (10 oz.) **Kraft® Cracker Barrel Sharp Cheddar Cheese,** red foil, grated
Chopped **Walnuts**

Mix all ingredients, forming a ball. Roll in walnuts.

Appetizers

Tex-Mex Dip

3 **Avocados**
2 tsp. **Lemon Juice**
1 cup **Sour Cream**
1 cup **Mayonnaise**
1 package (1.25 oz.) **Taco Seasoning**
Lettuce, shredded
2 cans (9 oz. each) **Bean Dip**
2 to 3 **Tomatoes**
1 can (6 oz.) sliced **Pitted Ripe Olives**
1 bunch **Green Onions**
8 oz. grated **Cheddar Cheese**
Tostados Chips for dipping

Peel and mash avocados with lemon juice, set aside. Combine sour cream, mayonnaise and taco seasonings. On serving platter shred lettuce. Layer the bean dip straight from the can. Next layer avocado mixture. Next layer with sour cream mixture. Sprinkle chopped onions, chopped tomatoes and olives. Add shredded cheese.

MAIN DISHES

In our American culture when we think of a main dish we think along the lines of some type of meat. Other cultures, based on religious or philosophical thought, stick to vegetables and grains. We know that the earliest of peoples cooked fresh kills over a fire and even shellfish have been recovered from both Neanderthal and Homo Sapiens excavations. We love meat! It's that simple. Grandma, in our more recent generations, has experimented enough to provide some classic recipes that are enough to make us howl!

Main Dishes

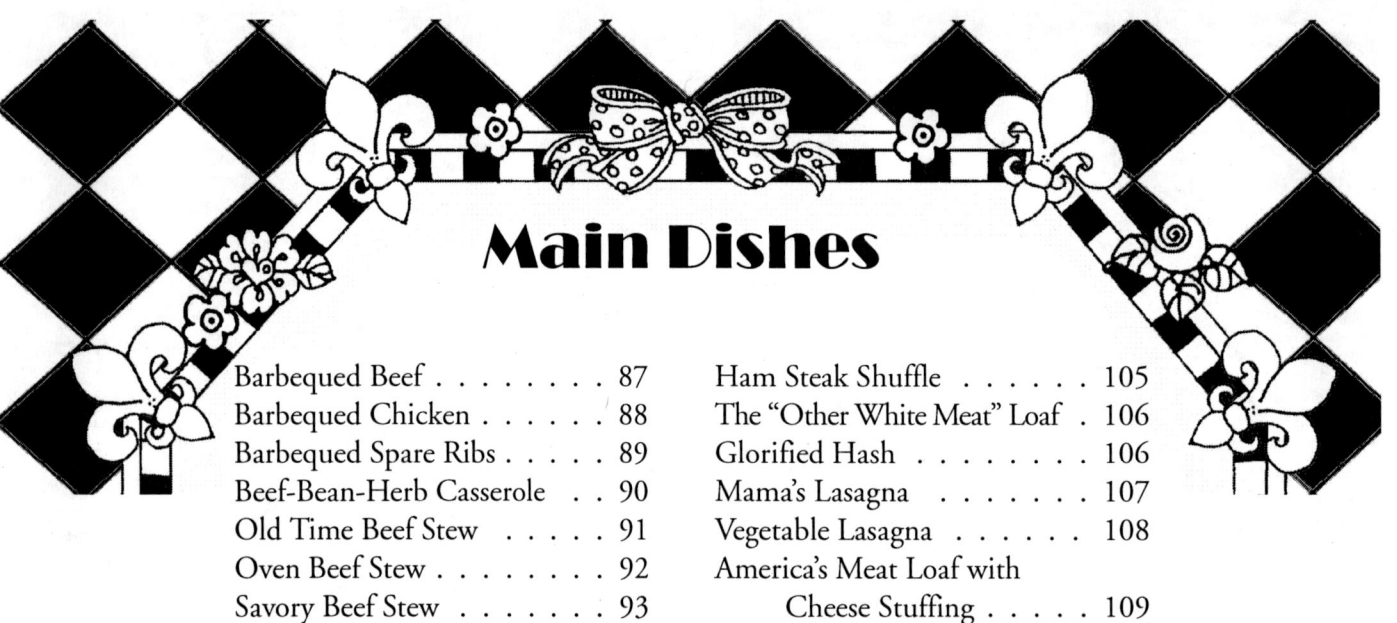

Barbequed Beef 87
Barbequed Chicken 88
Barbequed Spare Ribs 89
Beef-Bean-Herb Casserole . . 90
Old Time Beef Stew 91
Oven Beef Stew 92
Savory Beef Stew 93
Chicken Breasts in Parmesan
    Cream 93
Nana's Nuked Chicken
    and Dumplings 94
Beef Stroganoff 95
Stuffed Chicken Breasts 96
Southern Mother's Chicken
    Fried Steak. 97
Herb Roasted Chicken 98
Chicken and Lima Bean Stew . 99
Chicken Noodle Dish 100
Chicken Paprikash 100
Chicken Pie with Crust . . . 101
Elegant Chicken Pilaf 102
Chicken and Rice Skillet . . 103
"Grandma Has a Sore Back"
    Chicken-N-Rice 103
Fried Chicken in Sour Cream-
    Sherry Sauce 104
Walk The Flank Steak 105

Ham Steak Shuffle 105
The "Other White Meat" Loaf . 106
Glorified Hash 106
Mama's Lasagna 107
Vegetable Lasagna 108
America's Meat Loaf with
    Cheese Stuffing 109
Meat Loaf 110
Apple Meat Loaf 110
Uptown Manhattan Meat Loaf. . 111
Mel's Diner Pork Chop
    Casserole 112
Savory Pork Chops 112
Stuffed Pork Chops 113
Stuffed Pork Tenderloin . . . 114
Pork Chop Dinner 115
New England Pot Roast . . . 115
Pot Roast with Dumplings . . 116
Pot Roast with Golden Potatoes. 117
Shepherd's Pie 118
Easy Burgundy Stew. 119
Stuffed Cabbage Rolls. . . . 118
Sweet and Sour Pork 120
Tequila Chicken. 120

Barbequed Beef

2 to 3 lbs. **Stew Beef**	1 1/2 tsp. **Sugar**
1 tsp. **Pepper**	1 tsp. **Salt**
1 can (28 oz.) **Whole Peeled Tomatoes**	1 tsp. **Onion Salt**
	1 tsp. **Garlic Salt**
1 tsp. **Celery Salt**	1/2 cup **Chili Sauce**
1/2 bottle (14 oz.) **Ketchup**	1/2 cup **Vinegar**
2 tsp. **Worcestershire Sauce**	(More spices may be added to taste)

Cover stew beef with water and boil 10 to 15 minutes.

Then add all above ingredients. Bring to a boil again and then lower to a simmer and cook for 4 hours (or longer if needed). More water may be added while simmering, as needed. After allotted time take off the heat and use a potato masher to break up the meat. Serve on buns or rolls.

The history of barbeque or BBQ (or any of the many variations of the spelling) is as varied and vague as the name itself. Dating back thousands of years many cultures discovered the benefits of slow-cooking tough meats to create tasty meals. From digging pits for a Polynesian feast to creating a clambake in New England sand, slow-cooking food using smoky wood and hot rocks is an age-old method that lost its popularity until the late 1880s, in the American West. After a slight revival amongst early settlers in the late 17th century, who took their cue from native Indian cooking, frontiersmen in the Wild West started using BBQ techniques to help stretch an abundance of tough, gamey meats for all their workers and fellow ranch hands. Sauces soon followed to really flavor up the meal and, today, barbeque is a favorite past time for those friendly get-togethers. Although it's usually burly men we seem to conjure up when we picture eatin' good ol' barbeque, it was more than likely the women who did the most experimenting in the kitchen to find the best (or at least the easiest) way to create good-tasting food. Leave it to Grandma to feed the hands.

Barbequed Chicken

Sauce:

    1/3 cup **Cider Vinegar** or juice of 2 **Lemons**
    1/2 tsp. **Onion Salt** or juice of 1 **Onion**
    Dash of **Paprika**
    1 tbsp. **Tomato Paste**
    1 tsp. **Kitchen Bouquet**®
    1/2 tsp. **Salt**
    1/2 cup melted **Butter**
    1 tsp. **Worcestershire Sauce**
    1/8 tsp. **Pepper**
    Dash of **Garlic**

    3 **Chickens**, halved, washed and patted dry

Combine sauce ingredients and cook over low heat for 10 minutes. Remove from heat; set aside.

Salt, pepper and wrap chicken halves in aluminum foil, sealing well to prevent loss of juices. Bake in 350 degree oven on rimmed baking sheet or place chicken packages over open charcoal fire for at least 1 hour. Remove foil and continue baking for 15 minutes, basting each chicken half at least 3 times with sauce.

Barbequed Spare Ribs

2 lbs. **Pork Spare Ribs**
1/2 tsp. **Salt**
1/2 tsp. **Pepper**
2 tbsp. **Olive Oil**
1/3 cup minced **Onions**
1/2 cup diced **Celery**
1 clove **Garlic**, grated
1 tbsp. **Brown Sugar**
2 tsp. **Prepared Mustard**
2 tbsp. **Worcestershire Sauce**
2 tsp. **Lemon Juice**
Dash **Tabasco® Sauce**
1 can (10.75 oz.) **Campbell's® Tomato Soup**

Preheat oven to 250 degrees.

Season spare ribs with salt and pepper and roast for 2 hours. Remove from oven. Fire up a grill or your oven broiler. Melt shortening. Add onion and celery. Cook for 5 minutes. Add remaining ingredients. Cook 5 more minutes. Uncover spare ribs that have been baked for 1 hr. and soak spare ribs in the barbeque sauce, then broil or grill until brown.

This is as casserole as casserole gets...

Beef-Bean-Herb Casserole

1 lb. **Ground Chuck**
1 large **Onion,** chopped
2 cloves **Garlic**
1 **Green Pepper,** chopped
1/4 cup **Cooking Oil**
1 tbsp. **Flour**
2 cups **Canned Tomatoes,** drained, or **Fresh Tomatoes**
1/2 tsp. **Oregano**
1/4 tsp. **Thyme**
3 cans (15 oz.) **Kidney Beans,** drained
2 tbsp. chopped **Parsley**
1 tsp. **Salt**
1 tsp. **Sugar**
1/2 tsp. **Pepper**
1/8 tsp. ground **Cloves**
1/2 cup shredded **Cheese**

Preheat oven to 350 degrees.

Form ground beef into balls the size of walnuts. Sauté 1 large chopped onion, 2 cloves garlic, 1 chopped green pepper in 1/4 cup oil in large skillet. Push vegetables to side of pan and sauté meatballs until browned. Gently mix meat and vegetables together. Sprinkle 1 tbsp. flour over mixture and add all remaining ingredients except cheese. Bring to a gentle boil, then put in casserole and bake for about 40 minutes. Sprinkle with 1/2 cup shredded cheese and bake 5 minutes longer.

Serves 6 generously. Freezes well.

Old Time Beef Stew

2 tbsp. **Fat/Oil**	1/2 tsp. **Paprika**
2 lbs. **Beef Chuck**, cut in 1 1/2 inch cubes	1 or 2 **Bay Leaves**
1 large sliced **Onion**	Dash of **Allspice** or **Cloves**
1 clove **Garlic**	6 Medium **Potatoes**, diced
1 tbsp. **Lemon Juice**	6 **Carrots,** cut in quarters
4 cups **Boiling Water**	1 lb. **Small White Onions** (or Pearl Onions), trimmed and peeled
1 tbsp. **Salt**	
1 tsp. **Sugar**	
1 tsp. **Worcestershire Sauce**	1/4 cup **Flour**
1/2 tsp. **Pepper**	1/2 cup **Cold Water**

First: Heat oil on medium heat. Add beef chuck; brown on all sides, turning cubes with tongs. This should take about 20 minutes. Add onion slices, along with garlic. Add lemon juice and scrape up all the brown bits on the bottom of pan. Now add boiling water, salt, sugar, Worcestershire sauce, pepper, paprika, bay leaf, and allspice or cloves.

Second: Gentle cooking is what makes the meat tender, so cover and simmer (not boil) 2 hours. (Stir now and then to prevent sticking). Add the potatoes, carrots, and onions. Now simmer the stew about 30 minutes longer or till everything in the kettle is tender. Discard the bay leaf and garlic clove.

Third: Gravy time. Pour cold water into a shaker then add flour; shake hard to blend. Remove from heat, push the meat and vegetables to one side of pan; stir in flour mixture. Cook, stirring constantly, till the gravy thickens and boils. Reduce heat and cook gently about 10 minutes more. No lumps!

This stew will serve 6 to 8 hungry people. Serve while piping hot with fresh bread or biscuits.

Oven Beef Stew

1 1/2 lbs. **Lean Beef Stew Meat**
1/4 cup **Flour**
1/2 tsp. **Ground Black Pepper**
3 tsp. **Salt**, divided use
1 can (14.5 oz.) **Whole Peeled Tomatoes**
1/2 cup **Celery Flakes**
3 tbsp. **Onion Flakes**
1 tsp. **Basil Leaves**
1 tsp. **Tarragon**
8 **Potatoes**, cut in half
8 **Carrots**, cut in half
2 1/2 cups **Fresh Mushrooms**, sliced or 1 can (6 oz.) **Sliced Mushrooms**
3 tbsp. **Flour**
3 tbsp. **Water**

Preheat oven to 325 degrees.

Trim and reserve fat from meat. Cut into 1 1/2 inch cubes. Combine flour, pepper, and 1 tsp. salt. Sprinkle over meat. Brown meat in reserved fat. Turn into a 3-1/2 quart casserole. Combine tomatoes, remaining salt, celery, onions, herbs, potatoes, and carrots. Pour over meat. Cover and cook at for 2 hrs. Add mushrooms. Blend flour with water until smooth; stir in. Return to oven for 25 minutes.

Savory Beef Stew

2 lb. **Lean Cubed Chuck**
2 tsp. **Salt**
1 medium **Onion**
1 stalk **Celery**

1 can (10.75 oz.) **Condensed Tomato Soup**
8 **Carrots** (halved)
Salt and **Pepper** to taste
Pinch of **Whole Thyme**
Pinch of **Marjoram** or **Oregano**

Place meat in 2 or 3 quart pot and cover with cold water. Add about 2 tsp. salt and celery and onion, cut into small pieces. Cover and simmer about 50 minutes. Add soup, carrots, herbs, and more water and salt if needed. Simmer 45 minutes or until carrots are tender. Potatoes may be added for the last half hour. A can of small white onions (drained) may be added the last 10 minutes and then thicken with flour and water.

Serves 4-6

Chicken Breasts In Parmesan Cream

4 **Chicken Breast** halves
4 large stalks **Celery**, chopped
4 small **Tomatoes**, chopped
1 tbsp. chopped **Fresh Tarragon**
2/3 cup freshly grated **Parmesan Cheese**
2 cups **Heavy Cream**
Salt and **Pepper**
Dash of **Paprika**

Preheat oven to 350 degrees.

Arrange the chicken breasts in a large baking pan. Top with half of the cheese. Surround with the chopped vegetables, and sprinkle with salt, pepper, and the tarragon. Pour the cream over all, and top with the rest of the cheese. Sprinkle with paprika. Bake for 50 minutes. Serve over rice.

Nana's Nuked Chicken and Dumplings

(Nobody said every recipe had to be done the old-fashioned way)

3 lbs. **Chicken Parts**	2 **Bay Leaves**
3 small **Onions**, quartered	2 1/2 tsp. **Salt**
4 medium **Carrots**, cut into 1-in. pieces	1/4 tsp. **Thyme**
4 **Parsley** sprigs	1/4 tsp. **Poultry Seasoning**
1 can (14 oz.) **Chicken Broth**	1/8 tsp. **Pepper**
2 cups **Water**	3 tbsp. **Cornstarch**

Dumplings:

1 cup **Biscuit Mix**	1/4 tsp. **Poultry Seasoning**
1/3 cup **Milk**	

Combine all ingredients except cornstarch. Put into a 4-quart dish. Microwave on high for 25 minutes. Remove chicken and bay leaves. Mix 3 tbsp. cornstarch with 1/3 cup water. Add to broth. Microwave uncovered 5 minutes on high, stirring every 1 1/2 to 2 minutes until thickened. Remove bones from chicken, cut into bite-size pieces. Add to broth. Combine dumplings ingredients. Drop on chicken broth. Microwave high, 5 to 6 minutes, covered.

Beef Stroganoff

2 lbs. **Beef Tenderloin** or **Sirloin Steak**
1/4 cup **Butter** or **Margarine**
1 can (6 oz) sliced **Mushrooms**, drained
2 cans (10-1/2 oz. each) **Condensed Beef Broth** (bouillon)
1/3 cup instant minced **Onion**
1/4 cup **Teriyaki Soy Sauce**
1 1/2 tsp. **Garlic Salt**
1/3 cup **Flour**
2 cups **Dairy Sour Cream**
8 to 10 oz. uncooked medium **Noodles**
3 tbsp. **Butter** or **Margarine**

Cut meat across the grain into 3/4 inch slices, then into strips 3 x 1/4 inches. Melt 1/4 cup butter in large skillet. Cook and stir mushrooms in butter about 5 minutes; remove mushrooms. In same skillet, brown meat. Reserving 2/3 cup of the broth, stir in remaining broth, the onion, teriyaki soy sauce and garlic salt. Cover and simmer 15 minutes. Blend reserved broth and the flour; stir into meat. Add mushrooms; heat to boiling, stirring constantly. Boil and stir one minute. Stir in sour cream; heat through. Cook noodles as directed on package; drain. Toss with 3 tbsp. butter. Serve with stroganoff.

Serves 6 to 8

Stuffed Chicken Breasts

If you like chicken and you're in the mood for a relatively low-fat meal (you could always omit the cheese) give this a try.

  4 **Chicken Breasts**, skinless and boneless
  4 tbsp. **Honey**
  6-8 slices **Cheddar Cheese**
  4 oz. fresh **Basil**, chopped
  Handful of sliced **Almonds**
  Handful of **Raisins**
  One **Green Apple**, cored, peeled, and chopped
  Cinnamon
  Pepper
  Fresh **Rosemary**, chopped

All of the ingredients, unless specified, are to taste. Preheat oven to 375 degrees.

Place the chicken breasts on a piece of waxed paper. Cover with another sheet. Pound the chicken until it is no more than 1/4 inch high. Lightly spray some oil on a baking sheet covered with tin foil and place chicken on pan. Lightly coat the chicken with one tablespoon of honey. Be careful not to use too much, excess will burn. Add a thin slice or two of cheddar cheese. Sprinkle basil over the cheese. Place some almonds, raisins, and chopped apple on top of each breast. Sprinkle to taste with cinnamon, pepper and rosemary. Fold the sides of the breast and tuck in each end.

Stuff the chicken breasts on the conservative side; otherwise the breasts will be difficult to fold and the filling will fall out. Fasten together with toothpicks. (If the chicken is not overstuffed, this will be accomplished smoothly.) Bake the chicken on the upper level of the oven for approximately 40 minutes.

Serves 4

Southern Mother's Chicken Fried Steak

4 **Cubed Beef Steaks**
Salt
Pepper
1 cup **Flour**
1 **Egg**
1 tbsp. **Milk**
1 package of **Keebler® Club Crackers, Butter Crackers** or **Saltines**
1/3 cup **Vegetable Oil**

For gravy:

3 tbsp. **Rendered Fat** (bacon, beef, chicken, etc. or use butter)
1/2 cup finely diced **Onion**
3 tbsp. **Flour**
2 cups **Cream**
1/4 cup chopped fresh **Parsley** for garnish

Cut steak into individual serving-sized pieces. Sprinkle both sides with salt and pepper. Put pieces and flour into a plastic bag, seal the bag, and shake until the steak pieces are coated with flour. Whip egg and milk together and set aside. Place crackers in a plastic sealed bag and crush. Dip floured steak in the egg-milk mixture and then roll it in the crackers. Heat oil in an electric skillet at 350 degrees. Add steak and brown until blood no longer bleeds through steak. Remove steak to a serving plate and tent with foil to keep warm.

Meanwhile, sauté onion in fat or butter until translucent. (At this stage you can opt to add 1/4 cup dry white wine for a more refined flavor for the gravy or disregard it for a more traditional serving. If using the wine, let it reduce for at least 3 minutes to concentrate flavor.) Add the flour and simmer mixture on a low-medium heat until golden, about 5-6 minutes. Whisk in (slowly) the two cups of cream until desired consistency. Season with salt and pepper and serve with steak. Garnish with parsley.

Herb Roasted Chicken

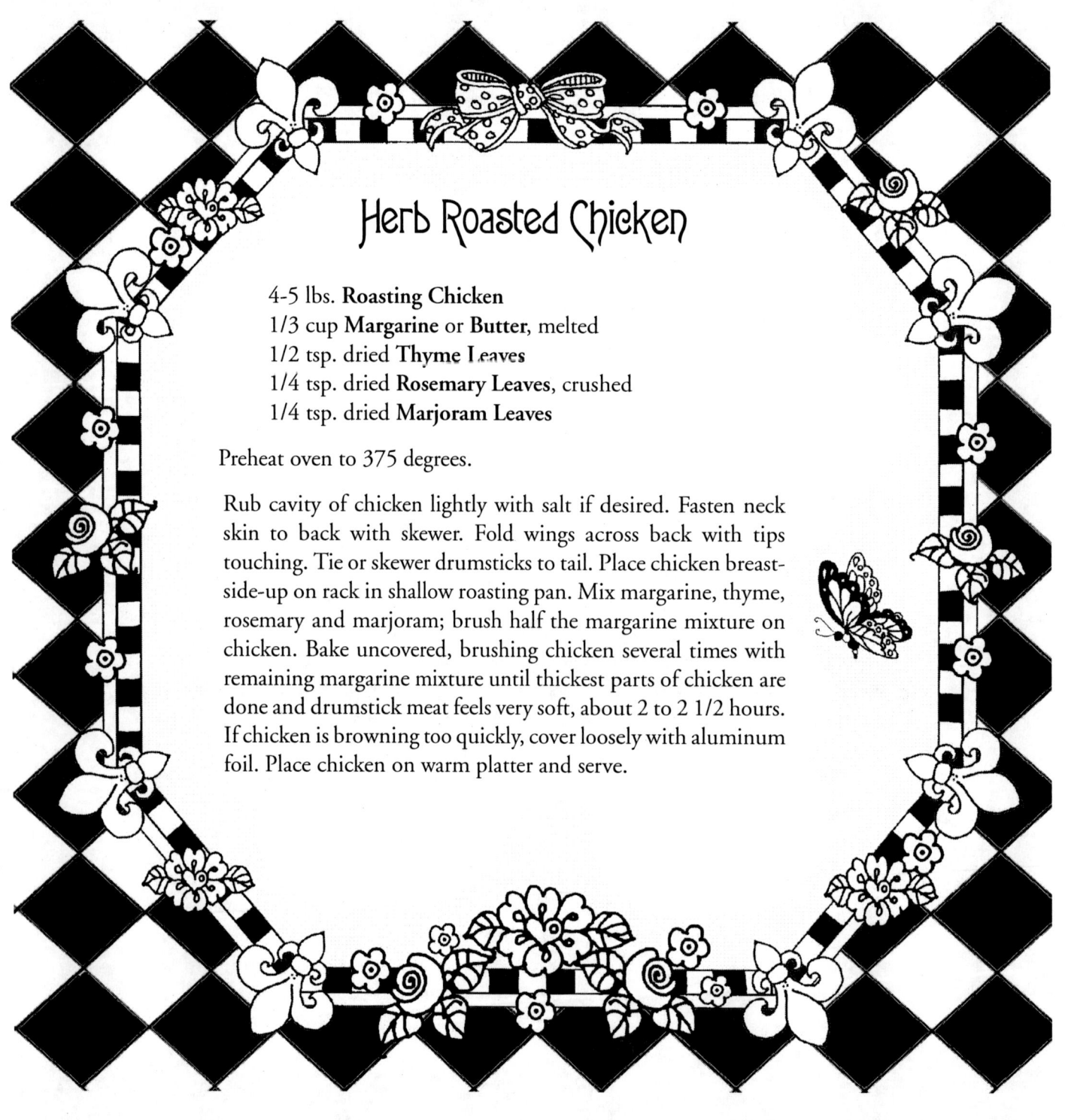

4-5 lbs. **Roasting Chicken**
1/3 cup **Margarine** or **Butter**, melted
1/2 tsp. dried **Thyme Leaves**
1/4 tsp. dried **Rosemary Leaves**, crushed
1/4 tsp. dried **Marjoram Leaves**

Preheat oven to 375 degrees.

Rub cavity of chicken lightly with salt if desired. Fasten neck skin to back with skewer. Fold wings across back with tips touching. Tie or skewer drumsticks to tail. Place chicken breast-side-up on rack in shallow roasting pan. Mix margarine, thyme, rosemary and marjoram; brush half the margarine mixture on chicken. Bake uncovered, brushing chicken several times with remaining margarine mixture until thickest parts of chicken are done and drumstick meat feels very soft, about 2 to 2 1/2 hours. If chicken is browning too quickly, cover loosely with aluminum foil. Place chicken on warm platter and serve.

Chicken and Lima Bean Stew

3 lbs. **Chicken**, cut up
3 1/4 cups **Water**
2 tsp. **Salt**
1 large **Potato**, cubed
1 medium **Onion**, chopped
1/4 tsp. **Ground Cumin**
1/4 tsp. **Black Pepper**
Dash of **Cayenne Pepper**
1 can (15.25 oz.) **Whole Kernel Corn**, undrained
1 can (14.5 oz.) **Whole Tomatoes**, undrained
1 package (10 oz.) **Frozen Lima Beans**
1 medium **Green Pepper**, diced
2 tbsp. **Flour**

Remove any excess fat from chicken. Heat chicken, giblets, neck, 3 cups of water and the salt to boiling in Dutch oven; reduce heat. Cover and simmer until thickest pieces of chicken are done, about 45 minutes. Skim fat from liquid if necessary. Remove chicken from bones if desired. Stir in potato, onion, cumin, pepper, cayenne pepper, corn, tomatoes and beans; break up tomatoes with fork. Heat to boiling; reduce heat. Cover and simmer 15 minutes. Add green pepper; cover and simmer until potato is tender, 5 to 10 minutes longer. Shake 1/4 cup water and the flour in tightly covered container. Stir into stew. Heat to boiling, stirring constantly. Boil and stir 1 minute.

Classic Chicken Noodle Dish

1 package (16 oz) medium width **Noodles**
2 cups **Tomato Juice**
1 **Onion**, diced and sautéed well
1 cup diced **Celery**, sautéed with onion
1 large box (2 lbs.) **Velveeta® Cheese**
1 can (10.75 oz.) condensed **Cream of Mushroom Soup**
1 can (4.25 oz.) chopped **Ripe Olives**
3 to 6 **Eggs**, hard-boiled and finely chopped
2 cups cooked, chopped **White Chicken**
Saltines

Cook noodles, drain and combine with other ingredients. Cover with a few crushed saltines. Bake at 350 degrees for 30 to 45 minutes until bubbly.

Chicken Paprikash

1 tbsp. **Margarine**
1/2 cup chopped **Onion**
3 1/2 lbs. **Frying Chicken**
Paprika, to taste

1 **Bay Leaf**
1 1/2 tsp. **Salt**
1 cup **Water**
8 oz. **Sour Cream**

Melt margarine. Add onions and cook over a very low heat until onions lose crispness. Pull onions to one side of pan. Add chicken that has been cut up. Sprinkle heavily with paprika until chicken is well coated. Add bay leaf, salt and water. Cover tightly. Cook slowly for 45 minutes or until chicken is tender. Add water when necessary to prevent sticking. Spoon sour cream over chicken; cover and cook slowly for 8 to 10 minutes. Stir sour cream into the paprika sauce and serve.

Chicken Pie with Crust

2 cut-up **Broiler / Fryers**
1 large **Onion**, quartered
4 **Carrots**, scraped, cut into pieces
2-3 cups **Water**
1/4 tsp. **Rosemary**
1/2 tsp. **Thyme**

1/4 tsp. **Marjoram**
2 tsp. **Salt**
1 tsp. **Pepper**
1 package (10 oz.) **Frozen Peas**, thawed
1/3 cup **Butter**
1/3 cup **Flour**
1 cup **Cream**

Preheat oven to 350 degrees.

Put chicken into stockpot with onion and carrots. Add water to cover. Add rosemary, thyme, marjoram, 1 tsp. salt and 1/2 tsp. pepper. Bring to boil and simmer covered, for about 45 minutes or until chicken is cooked. Drain chicken and vegetables, reserve broth. Remove bones and skin from chicken pieces and cut meat into bite-sized chunks. Return chicken to reserved vegetables; add peas. Remove 1 1/2 cups broth from pot. Melt butter in saucepan and blend in flour. Gradually add hot broth and cream, stirring constantly until thickened and smooth. Add remaining 1 tsp. salt and 1/2 tsp. pepper. Pour sauce over chicken and vegetables, adding more broth if necessary.

Pastry:

1 cup **Shortening**
3 cups **Flour**

1/2 tsp. **Salt**
1/2- 3/4 cup **Cold Water**
Milk for brushing

Cut shortening into flour mixed with salt. Add water. Mix well to form ball. Roll out top and bottom crusts. Place bottom crust in 9" deep-dish pie plate. Pour in chicken mixture and cover with top crust. Brush with milk.

Pierce three small holes in top crust to let steam escape and put ring of foil around edge to prevent over-browning. Bake for 35-40 minutes, or until brown, removing aluminum foil after about 10 minutes. Serves 6-8.

(Don't hesitate to use store-bought pie crusts. Cheating is okay and they taste almost as good as Grandma's.)

Main Dishes

Elegant Chicken Pilaf Soup

4 to 5 lb. **Roasting Chicken**	3/4 tsp. **Mace**
1/3 cup **Flour**	1/2 tsp. **Chili Powder**
1/3 cup **Butter**	3/4 cup **Flaked Coconut**
2 **Onions**, peeled	1 **Bay Leaf**, crumbled
4 **Carrots**	2 cans (14 oz. each) **Chicken Broth**
2 stalks **Celery**	3 cups **Water**
2 tart **Apples**	1 cup **Apple Juice**
1 1/2 tbsp. **Curry Powder**	1 cup **Light Cream**
4 tsp. **Salt**	**Elegant Pilaf**

(I know this is a soup, but its preparation and final result is so regal it qualifies as a full-blown meal.)

Cut chicken into pieces and roll in flour; reserve remaining flour. Chop onion, slice carrots and celery, peel, core, and dice apples. Brown chicken in hot butter in a heavy pot until browned on all sides. Remove chicken. In skillet, add onion, carrot, celery, apple, remaining flour, curry, salt, mace, chili powder, coconut and bay leaf. Cook, stirring for 5 minutes. Add broth and 3 cups water and return chicken to pan. Simmer, covered, 2 hours, stirring occasionally. Remove from heat and refrigerate overnight. Next day skim fat from surface of soup. Remove skin and bone from chicken and cut meat into large pieces; return to pot. Add apple juice and cream and reheat just before serving.

Serve with Elegant Pilaf.

Elegant Pilaf

1 cup regular **White Rice**	1/4 tsp. **Cinnamon**
1/2 cup **Seedless Raisins**	Dash **Mace**
1/4 cup slivered and toasted **Almonds**	1/3 cup chopped **Parsley**

Cook rice using package directions. Combine rice, raisins, almonds, cinnamon and mace; toss gently. To serve, spoon pilaf into warm bowls. Add soup and garnish with parsley. Serves 8.

"Before There Were Crockpots" Chicken and Rice

1 1/2 tsp. **Turmeric Powder**
2 cups **Flour**
2 1/2 lbs. **Chicken**, cut up
Olive Oil
1 cup chopped **Onion**
1/2 cup diced **Green Pepper**
1/2 chopped **Red Pepper**
2 small cloves **Garlic**
1 cup uncooked **Rice**
2 cups **Chicken Broth** or stock
1 tsp. **Salt**
Pepper to taste

Preheat oven to 220 degrees.

Combine turmeric powder and flour. Roll cut-up chicken in seasoned flour. Add olive oil to dutch oven and brown chicken. Remove from skillet. Add onion to skillet and cook until transparent (about 7 minutes). Then, add green and red pepper, garlic and rice. Stir at low heat for 2 minutes. Add broth; place chicken on top of rice mixture. Cover and bake for 75 minutes.

"Grandma Has A Sore Back" Chicken-N-Rice

(This is a glorified throw-together meal that is so easy to prepare it's silly.)

1 can (10.75 oz.) **Cream of Mushroom Soup**
1 can (10.75 oz.) **Cream of Celery Soup**
1 1/3 cups **Milk**
6 **Chicken Thighs**, pieced
1/2 envelope **of Onion Soup Mix**
1 1/3 cup **Instant Rice**

Preheat oven to 325 degrees.

In saucepan heat together the soup and milk. Mix in instant rice. Pour mixture into greased casserole or baking dish. Place chicken pieces on top. Sprinkle 1/2-envelope onion soup mix on top. Seal with aluminum foil or cover. Bake for 3 hours.

Fried Chicken In Sour Cream-Sherry Sauce

8 pieces **Chicken** (breast halves and thighs)
Salt and **Pepper** to taste
1 tbsp. **Butter**
2 cups **Milk**
Fresh chopped **Parsley** to taste or dried **Parsley Flakes**
1/4 cup **Dry Sherry**
1 cup **Sour Cream**

Remove skin from chicken and season with salt and pepper. Brown lightly in butter in deep skillet. Cover with milk and cook very slowly until tender (30 minutes). If it cooks down, baste with milk from pan. Add parsley and sherry. Cook for 5 to 10 additional minutes. Remove chicken to serving platter, keep hot. Stir sour cream into pan juices. Heat, but do not boil. Pour sauce over chicken and serve with boiled potatoes or rice. Serves 3 to 4.

Browning butter is a delicate task. Heat butter over a low-medium heat until it bubbles and browns. Remove the pan from heat immediately, since there is a very fine line between brown butter and burnt butter. Burnt butter, like burnt garlic, will ruin any dish you prepare. If it happens, do your guests a favor…start over.

Ham Steak Shuffle

2 tbsp. melted **Butter**
2 cups **Whole Wheat Bread Crumbs**
2/3 cup diced **Apples**
1/3 cup **Seedless Raisins**
1/2 cup **Half & Half**
2 large slices cooked **Ham Steaks**
6 whole **Cloves**
3 tbsp. **Brown Sugar**

Preheat oven to 325 degrees.

Melt butter; mix in breadcrumbs, apples and raisins, mixing well. Moisten with half and half. Mix together. Place 1 slice of ham in a greased casserole dish. Spread with the stuffing mixture. Top with another slice of ham. (If ham is not already cooked, cooking time must be longer.) Stick cloves into the top slice of ham. Sprinkle with the brown sugar. Cover and bake in a slow oven 40 minutes or until tender. Serves 4.

"Walk The Flank" Steak

1 to 2 lbs. **Flank Steak**
Sea Salt
1/4 tsp. **Ground Ginger**
1/4 tsp. **Garlic Powder**
1/2 cup **Soy Sauce**
1/4 cup **Honey**
Pepper, to taste

Sprinkle the steak with sea salt before you prepare remaining recipe. Mix all ingredients except the steak, and pour mixture over the flank steak in a glass dish. Marinate the steak in the marinade for 4 to 8 hours, turning meat occasionally. (It's even better marinated overnight!) Grill the meat about 10 minutes on each side for medium rare. Slice thin with an electric knife, against the grain of the meat.

The "Other White Meat" Loaf

1 cup **Whole Wheat Bread Crumbs**
1/4 cup **Half & Half**
1 **Egg**, slightly beaten
2 lbs. ground uncooked **Ham**
1 lb. **Ground Pork Shoulder** (have butcher grind)
1/8 tsp. **Pepper**

1 tbsp. **Vinegar**
1 tsp. **Prepared Mustard**
1/4 cup **Brown Sugar**
1 tbsp. melted **Butter**

Preheat oven to 350 degrees.

Soften breadcrumbs in half & half. Add slightly beaten egg. Add meats and pepper. Form into loaf. Line a loaf pan with wax paper. Fill loaf pan with meat mixture. Chill.

Remove meatloaf from pan and remove wax paper. Place inverted in shallow baking pan and baste with sauce made by heating vinegar, mustard, brown sugar, and butter in saucepan, until sugar is slightly melted. Bake ham loaf 1 1/2 hours.

Can be divided into two smaller loaves. Freeze one for a future meal, or slice cold for marvelous sandwiches. Substitute ground ham with beef if it's easier.

Glorified Hash

This versatile dish is good served for breakfast (with hot rolls and fruit), lunch (with a salad), or supper (with a vegetable). We didn't think one can of hash could provide six servings. In this recipe, it does! Holy hash!

1 can (15 oz.) **Corned Beef Hash**
1 cup **Shredded Cheese**
2 **Eggs**, beaten
1 1/4 cups **Milk**

1 pinch each of **Nutmeg** and **Dry Mustard**
1 tbsp. **Flour**
1/4 each of **Salt** and **Pepper**

Crumble hash in casserole or 9 x 9 inch pan and sprinkle with cheese. Mix remaining ingredients and pour over. Bake 35 minutes or until custard is set. Cool slightly so pieces stay intact when you cut them.

Mama's Lasagna

I'm not Italian and will never pretend to be (except after I watch The Godfather movies and for a couple of days, everything is badda-bing, badda-boom). But if there is ever a chance to make this dish from my friend Joey's family archive, take that chance. We're so used to preparing pasta dishes these days that begin with opening a can or a jar that we forget the depth of flavor that comes from using fresh ingredients. Now, get in the kitchen, pronto!

1/2 cup **Water**	1 tsp. **Dried Basil Leaves**
1/2 cup chopped **Onion**	1 tsp. **Salt**
1 cup chopped **Celery**	6 **Lasagna Noodles**
1 clove **Garlic,** crushed	1 1/2 cups **Dry Cottage Cheese**
1/2 lb. **Ground Beef**	1 **Egg**
1 can (14 oz.) **Italian Plum Tomatoes**	8 oz. **Mozzarella Cheese,** cut in 6 slices
1 can (6 oz.) **Tomato Paste**	1 tbsp. **Parmesan Cheese**
1/4 cup chopped **Parsley**	**Paprika,** optional
2 tsp. **Dried Oregano Leaves**	

Preheat oven to 350 degrees.

In large skillet, combine 1/2 cup water, onion, celery, and garlic. Cook over medium heat until tender and water has evaporated—about 10 minutes. Add ground beef, and sauté until browned. Stir in tomatoes, tomato paste, parsley, oregano, basil, and salt. Bring to boil; reduce heat and simmer for 20 minutes, uncovered, stirring occasionally.

Cook noodles as package label directs. Combine cottage cheese and egg in small bowl; stir until well blended. Place 3 noodles in bottom of lightly greased, 10 x 6 x 2 baking dish. Top with half of cottage cheese mixture, then half of meat sauce; repeat. Arrange mozzarella on top, sprinkle with Parmesan and paprika.

Bake uncovered 30 minutes or until very hot and golden brown. Let Lasagna stand 10 minutes before serving.

Vegetable Lasagna

1/4 tbsp. **Vegetable Oil**
1 1/4 tbsp. finely chopped **Onion**
1 clove **Garlic**, minced
2 cup **Tomato Sauce**
1/2 tsp. crushed **Oregano Leaves**
2 2/3 cups **Ricotta Cheese**
2 2/3 tbsp. grated **Parmesan Cheese**
2 tbsp. chopped **Fresh Parsley**
Dash of **Pepper**
2 cups sliced **Zucchini**
8 oz. **Lasagna Noodles**, cooked, drained

Preheat oven to 400 degrees.

To prepare sauce, heat oil in a medium saucepan. Add onion and garlic and sauté until soft. Add tomato sauce and oregano. Simmer 15 minutes to blend flavors. In a medium bowl, combine cheeses, parsley and pepper until well mixed; set aside. In a 9 x 12 baking dish, layer sauce, lasagna noodles, ricotta cheese mixture and zucchini, beginning and ending with sauce. Bake, covered with foil for 20 to 25 minutes. For a crisper top, remove foil after 15 minutes. Let stand for 10 minutes before serving.

America's Meat Loaf With Cheese Stuffing

4 **Eggs**
3 lb. **Chuck Beef**, ground once
3 cups fresh **Bread Crumbs**
1 cup minced **Onion**
1/2 cup minced **Green Pepper**
3 tbsp. **Horseradish**

1 tbsp. **Salt**
2 tbsp. **Prepared Mustard**
1/4 cup **Evaporated Milk**
1/4 cup **Ketchup**
2 packages (8 oz. each) sliced **Processed Sharp Cheese**
Snipped **Parsley**

Preheat oven to 400 degrees.

In a large bowl, beat eggs slightly with fork. Lightly mix in chuck, then crumbs, onion and green pepper. (Meat will be juicier and more tender if you handle it as little as possible.) Add horseradish, salt, mustard, milk and ketchup. Combine thoroughly with as few turns as possible. Divide meat mixture into 3 equal parts.

In bottom of 10 x 5 x 3 inch loaf pan, gently pat one part of meat mixture. Cover this with 5 overlapping cheese slices. Spread on second part of meat mixture. Repeat with 6 more cheese slices, then remaining meat mixture. Chill in refrigerator for 1 hour.

Invert loaf on jellyroll pan or foil covered cookie sheet (with latter, turn up foil edges to form rim). Bake 50 minutes. 5 minutes before end of baking time, crumble 2 cheese slices over top of meat loaf. When loaf is done, let it stand out of oven 15 minutes before serving. Serve sliced, hot or cold, with snipped parsley sprinkled on top.

Makes 10 to 12 servings.

Meat Loaf

1 1/2 lbs. **Ground Beef**
3/4 cup **Bread Crumbs**
1/2 cup chopped **Onion**
1 **Egg**
1 tsp. **Salt**

2 cans (8 oz. each) **Tomato Sauce**
1/2 cup **Parmesan Cheese**
1/2 tsp. **Oregano**
1/8 tsp. **Pepper**
1 1/2 cups shredded **Mozzarella Cheese**

Preheat oven to 350 degrees.

Mix all ingredients together, except cheese, reserving 1/2 cup tomato sauce (save remainder for topping). Tear off piece of foil to use as sheet to pat out meat mixture into 10 x 12 rectangle. Line flat pan using foil as a lifter—lift roll as jellyroll after sprinkling surface with cheese. Seal ends and place seam side down in pan. Bake 60 minutes. Remove from oven; pour off fat, top with remaining sauce. Bake 15 minutes more—let stand before cutting.

Apple Meat Loaf

An excellent twist with a hint of autumn taste built right in.

1 large **Onion**, finely chopped
2 tbsp. **Butter**
2 1/2 lbs. **Ground Beef**
1 1/2 cups fresh **Bread Crumbs**
2 cups finely chopped, peeled and cored **Apples**
3 **Eggs**, beaten

1 tbsp. chopped **Parsley**
1/2 tsp. **Pepper**
2 tsp. **Salt**
1/4 tsp. **Allspice**
1 tbsp. **Prepared Mustard** or
    1/4 tsp. **Dry Mustard**
1/4 cup **Ketchup**

Preheat oven to 350 degrees.

Sauté onion in butter until soft. Then combine all ingredients, mixing thoroughly. Form into loaf and place in 10 x 14 baking pan (or pack into large greased loaf pan). Bake for 1 hour. Remove from oven and let sit for 15 minutes before serving.

Serves 8-10.

Uptown Manhattan Meat Loaf

(If it weren't still a meat loaf they'd serve it at the Waldorf-Astoria)

1/3 lb. each **Lean Ground Beef**, **Pork** and **Veal**
1/2 tsp. **Parsley Flakes**
1/4 cup **Bread Crumbs**
1 tbsp. **Salad Oil**
1/4 cup minced **Onions**
1 tsp. **Salt**
2/3 cup sliced **Mushrooms**, canned, fresh or sautéed
Dash **Pepper**
1/4 cup **Milk**
1 **Egg**
1/2 tsp. **Dried Basil**
1/3 cup **Tomato Juice** or **Dry Red Wine**

Preheat oven to 325 degrees.

Mix all ingredients in a large mixing bowl. Place in lightly oiled loaf pan. Bake for about one hour or until meat thermometer reads 165 F. Makes about 6 servings. Leftover meatloaf can be used cold for sandwiches.

Mel's Diner Pork Chop Casserole

4 **Pork Chops**
1/2 cup **Raw Rice**
1 can (14 oz.) **Beef Broth**

4 thick slices **Onion**
4 slices **Tomato**
4 slices **Green Pepper**

Preheat oven to 350 degrees.

Brown the pork chops. In bottom of glass oven pan, place 1/2 cup rice and beef broth, then the pork chops. Place on top of each chop a thick slice of onion, tomato and green pepper. Season each layer. Bake for about 1 hour covered, until liquid is gone and rice is tender.

Savory Pork Chops
Microwave

6 medium **Pork Chops**
1 tbsp. minced **Onion**
1 tbsp. **Worcestershire Sauce**
1 can (10.75 oz.) **Cream of Mushroom Soup**
1 can (14 oz.) **Beef Broth** or **Pork Gravy**

Trim excess fat from chops.

Arrange pork chops in 8 x 12 inch Pyrex or glass baking dish, in one layer, if possible. Sprinkle with onion and Worcestershire. Pour undiluted soup over top. Cover with waxed paper. Microwave on high 18 minutes or until tender. For gravy, add a can of pork gravy or can of beef broth to mixture. Cook a minute or so longer.

Stuffed Pork Chops

1 large **Onion**, finely chopped
1/2 cup finely chopped **Celery**
1/4 cup chopped **Nuts**
2 tbsp. **Butter**
3/4 cup soft fresh **Bread Crumbs**
1/4 cup chopped **Parsley**
1/4 tsp. **Salt**
1/8 tsp. grated **Nutmeg**
1 **Egg**, lightly beaten
Freshly ground **Black Pepper**, to taste
6 **Double Loin Pork Chops** (consult the butcher if needed)
1 cup **Beef Stock**, optional

Preheat oven to moderate 350 degrees.

Sauté the onion, celery and nuts in the butter until the onion is soft. Remove from heat. Add the breadcrumbs, parsley, salt, nutmeg and egg to the onion mixture. Add pepper to taste. Mix well. Slice a pocket through center of loin on the chop and fill with stuffing. Place the chops in a shallow baking dish, cover with foil and bake for about 1 hour, turning chops after 30 minutes. Uncover and continue baking about 30 more minutes until well browned. Remove chops and keep warm.

If desired for sauce: drain any fat from the pan, add stock and heat, while scraping loose any browned particles that cling to the pan. Pour the sauce around the chops.

Note: Chops with bone may be used, and will require less cooking time. Chicken broth may be substituted for the beef broth.

Stuffed Pork Tenderloin

1 **Pork Tenderloin**
1 **Apple,** peeled, chopped
6 cooked, pitted **Prunes,** chopped
Salt and **Pepper**
2 tbsp. **Butter** or **Margarine**
2 cups **Chicken** or **Beef Broth**
1 cup **Heavy Cream**

Take tenderloin long-way and make a 3/4-inch deep gash from end to end. Open and flatten. Add apples and prunes, salt and pepper. Starting with narrowest end, roll like a jellyroll. Secure with kitchen string and brown on all sides in butter; add broth—cover and simmer for 1 hour. At halfway point add heavy cream. When done pour all pan juices into a blender, whirl until smooth and consistent, pour over meat.

Serves 3 to 4.

When using a blender to purée hot foods and sauces, only fill halfway, as the contents will expand due to the heat. If the blender starts full, it will result in quite a mess!

Pork Chop Dinner

1 tbsp. **Margarine**
8 **Lean Pork Chops**
2 medium **Onions**
1/2 tsp. **Salt**
1/4 tsp. **Curry Powder**
1 can (10.75 oz.) **Cream of Mushroom Soup**
1/4 can **Water**
4 medium **Potatoes**

Preheat oven to 325 degrees.

Melt margarine in large skillet. Brown pork chops approximately 5 minutes on each side. Remove from skillet. Brown onions thinly sliced and separated into rings. Combine salt and curry powder with soup diluted with water. Layer potatoes, pork chops and onion rings in a 2-quart casserole. Pour in soup mixture. Cover and bake for 30 minutes.

Serves 8.

New England Pot Roast

4 lbs. **Beef Arm Blade**
    or **Cross Rib Pot Roast**
1 tbsp. **Salt**
1 tsp. **Pepper**
5 oz. **Horseradish**
1 cup **Water**
8 small **Potatoes**, cut into halves
8 medium **Carrots**, cut into fourths
8 small **Onions**
1/2 cup **Cold Water**
1/4 cup **Flour**

Cook beef in Dutch oven over medium heat until brown; reduce heat. Sprinkle with salt and pepper. Spread horseradish over both sides of beef. Add 1 cup of water. Heat to boiling; reduce heat. Cover; simmer on top of range or cook in 325 degree oven for 2 1/2 hours. Add vegetables. Cover; cook until tender, about 1 hour. Remove to warm platter. Skim excess fat from broth. Add enough water to broth to measure 2 cups. Shake ½ cup cold water and the flour in tightly covered container; stir gradually into broth. Heat to boiling, stirring constantly. Boil and stir 1 minute. Serve gravy with beef.

Main Dishes 115

Pot Roast with Dumplings

Meat:

    2 lb. **Chuck Roast**   1/2 cup chopped **Onion**
    Salt and **Pepper**   1/4 tsp. **Garlic Salt**
    1/4 cup **Butter**   1 cup **Water**

Sauce:

    1/4 cup **Brown Sugar**   1/2 tsp. **Dry Mustard**
    2 tbsp. **Vinegar**   1/4 cup **Lemon Juice**
    1/4 cup **Chili Sauce**

Dumplings:

    1 cup **Whole Wheat Flour**   1/4 tsp. **Salt**
    1 tsp. **Baking Powder**   **Water** to mix
    1 **Egg**

Preheat oven to 325 degrees.

Rub the roast with salt and pepper. Brown on all sides in the butter melted in Dutch oven. Add onion and garlic salt, 1 cup of water; cover and cook slowly 1 hour. Combine the sauce ingredients together. Then, pour over meat and cook another hour, or until tender. Remove meat from sauce and keep hot.

For dumplings add the flour, baking powder and salt to whipped egg. Add only enough water to make stiff dough. Drop a teaspoon of the dumplings dough in the hot meat sauce. Cover tightly and steam 15 minutes, without removing lid.

6 generous servings.

Pot Roast with Golden Potatoes

A genuine old-time favorite.
Must be cooked in a heavy old-fashioned cast iron pot.

3 lbs. **Beef Round** or **Rump**	**Salt**
1 tsp. **Prepared Mustard**	**Pepper**
3 lbs. **Pork Shoulder**	2 cups plus 4 tbsp. **Cold Water**
1 clove **Garlic**	3 **Potatoes**, sliced
1 4 lb. **Chicken**	4 tbsp. **Cornstarch**
1 tsp. **Summer Savory**	

Preheat oven to 300 degrees.

Rub the beef with mustard, the pork with garlic and spread the summer savory on the chicken. Roast meat in a cast iron kettle for 3 hours. Remove the meat to a platter and place pot on high heat until liquid evaporates. Add 2 cups cold water and simmer for 10 minutes stirring and scraping the bottom. This liquid should be a golden color. Add potatoes and boil slowly turning them carefully with a spoon until golden brown. Remove potatoes to platter. Mix together 4 tablespoons cold water plus 4 tablespoons cornstarch. Whisk cornstarch mixture into hot liquid until thickened. Serve hot.

Shepherd's Pie

1 1/2 lbs. **Ground Beef**, cooked and drained
1 **Onion**, chopped
1 can (15.25 oz.) **Kernel Corn**
1 can (10.75 oz.) **Tomato Soup**
5 medium **Potatoes**, seasoned, cooked and mashed
Farmers Cheese or shredded **Cheddar**
Butter

Preheat oven to 300 degrees.

Grease a 2-quart casserole. Add ground beef and onion on bottom, corn in the middle. Pour soup over both layers and add potatoes on top. Sprinkle with desired cheese. Dot with butter and cook for 15 minutes or until potatoes start to brown.

This dish is best when prepared with quality ingredients. Use a good Idaho potato and splurge on the Farmers Cheese for a true authentic taste.

Stuffed Cabbage Rolls

12 large **Cabbage Leaves**
Boiling Water
1 1/4 lb. **Ground Beef**
2 tsp. **Salt**
1/2 tsp. **Pepper**
1 cup cooked **Rice**
1 small **Onion**, chopped
1 **Egg**, lightly beaten
1/2 tsp. **Poultry Seasoning** or **Thyme**
2 tbsp. **Vegetable Oil**
2 cans (8 oz. each) **Tomato Sauce**
2-4 tbsp. **Brown Sugar**
1/4 cup **Water**
1 tbsp. **Lemon Juice** or **Vinegar**

Cover cabbage leaves with boiling water and let stand for 5 minutes or until limp; drain and trim out rib. Combine next 7 ingredients. Place equal portions of the meat mixture in center of each leaf. Fold sides of each leaf over meat; roll up and fasten with toothpicks or string. Brown the rolls in hot oil in very large skillet. Pour in tomato sauce. Combine sugar, water and lemon juice. Stir into tomato sauce. Simmer filled cabbage rolls covered, one hour, basting occasionally.

Makes 6 servings.

Easy Burgundy Stew

2 cups sliced **Carrots**
1 cup sliced **Celery**
2 **Onions**, sliced
1 can (8 oz.) sliced **Water Chestnuts**
1 can (8 oz.) sliced **Mushrooms**, drained
3 tbsp. **Flour**
1 tsp. **Salt**
1 tsp. **Dried Thyme Leaves**
1 tsp. **Dry Mustard**
1/4 tsp. **Black Pepper**
2 lbs. **Beef Stew Meat**
1 cup **Water**
1 cup **Dry Red Wine**
1 can (14 oz.) **Whole Peeled Tomatoes**, drained

Preheat oven to 325 degrees.

Mix carrots, celery, onions, water chestnuts and mushrooms in Dutch oven or 4-quart casserole. In separate bowl, mix flour, salt, thyme, mustard and pepper. Coat beef with flour mixture. Place beef in Dutch oven on top of vegetables. Combine wine, water and tomatoes. Pour on top of beef. Cover and bake until beef is tender and stew is thickened, about 4 hours.

Simple Sweet and Sour Pork

3 lbs. **Pork Loin**, cubed
1/2 cup **Ketchup**
4 tbsp. **Soy Sauce**
4 tbsp. **Cornstarch**
1 clove **Garlic**
1/2 cup **Water**
1/2 cup **White Vinegar**
1/2 cup **Sugar**
4 tbsp. **Pineapple Juice**
1/2 **Bell Pepper**, diced
1 small **Onion**, chopped

Mix all ingredients together and bake, covered, in a 300-degree oven for 3 hours. (Or even better—in a crock pot on low all day—10 hours). Serve with rice. Great make-ahead dish.

Tequila Chicken

2 tbsp. **Olive Oil**
1 **Elephant Garlic Clove**, minced
2 **Anaheim Chile Peppers**, chopped
1 **Scallion** or **Small Onion**, chopped
4 skinless, boneless **Chicken Breast Halves**
Salt and **Pepper**
1/2 cup **Tequila**
Juice of 1 **Lime**
1 tbsp. chopped **Rosemary**
2 tbsp. **Butter**

Heat one tbsp. of the oil in a pan over medium heat. Add the garlic, peppers, and scallion. Cook until the garlic is soft. Remove the vegetables from the pan. Sprinkle the chicken with salt and pepper. Add the remaining oil to the pan and brown the chicken for about 3 minutes on each side. Add the tequila, lime juice, rosemary, and sautéed vegetables. Cover and simmer for about 5 minutes, until the chicken is no longer pink. Swirl in the butter and serve.

VEGETABLES & SIDES

The history of the side dish is actually rather boring. Some families, in fact, served veggies and sides as the main fare. Grandma knew the importance of a well-balanced meal, so naturally her main dish was always served with something to create a balance. Nowadays the side dish is a well thought out concept and chefs are incredibly particular about which food goes with another. As for Grandma…well, she still knows what's best for us. Here are a few of her favorites.

Vegetables and Sides

Baked Asparagus 123
Traditional Baked Beans . . . 124
Boston Baked Beans 125
California Baked Beans . . . 125
Baked Hominy 134
Beer Batter Fried Veggies
    'n' Things 126
Carrots Vichy 127
Corn Pudding 127
Country Hominy Grits . . . 128
Never Fail Dumplings 128
Giblet Bread Stuffing 130
Green Bean Casserole 129
Hush Puppies 131

Noodle and Cheese Kugel . . . 131
Noodle Pudding 132
Easy Potatoes Au Gratin 133
Shrimp-Stuffed Acorn Squash . 133
Sausage-Zucchini Boats 134
Spinach Pie 135
Spinach Parmesan 136
Succotash 136
Sweet Potato Casserole 137
Wild Rice-Mushroom Stuffing . 138

122 Grandma's Favorite Country Recipes

Baked Asparagus

    1 bunch **Asparagus**, blanched
    1 cup **Grated Cheese** divided (Parmesan, Swiss, Cheddar – choose your favorite)
    2 **Eggs**, hard-boiled and crumbled
    1 1/2 cups **Medium White Sauce** (recipe follows)
    1/4 cup melted **Butter**
    1 cup crushed **Corn Flakes**

Preheat oven to 350 degrees.

Lay asparagus in a clear or Pyrex® baking dish. Sprinkle cheese over top of asparagus. Top with crumbled eggs. Pour white sauce over asparagus. In bowl mix 1/4 cup melted butter with 1 cup of crushed corn flakes. Crumble buttered crushed corn flakes on top. Bake until crumbs are brown, about 25-30 minutes.

White Sauce:

    2 tbsp. **Butter**
    2 tbsp. **Flour**
    Salt and **Pepper**
    1 cup **Milk**

Melt butter in a pan and add flour to make a roux and simmer for several minutes to brown and take away the "floury" taste. Add salt and pepper and whisk in milk until desired consistency.

Traditional Baked Beans

12 cups **Beans**
2 cups **Brown Sugar**
2 tbsp. **Salt**
1/3 cup **Vinegar**
3 tbsp. **Molasses**
2 lbs. **Salt Pork** or **Bacon**
1 tsp. **Mustard**
Water as needed

Preheat oven to 325 degrees.

Soak 12 cups of beans. Then parboil in same water for 15-20 minutes. Drain. Put beans in large roaster pan. Mix remaining ingredients. Pour over beans. Bake all day or all night. Add water as needed.

Beans from scratch are an easy start, but need attention throughout the cooking process so they don't dry out and burn. When done correctly, beans are a delicious and very healthy alternative to potatoes and starches. When not attended to, however, you'll probably end up throwing out the pan. For your health, give them a try.

Boston Baked Beans

1 lb. **Dried Pea Beans**
2 cups **Water**
1/4 lb. piece **Salt Pork**
1 **Onion**, whole

1/2 cup **Molasses**
1 tsp. **Dry Mustard**
1/2 cup **Brown Sugar**
1 tsp. **Salt**

Soak beans overnight in water. Simmer in the same water for 15 minutes. Drain. Put half the salt pork in the bottom of a bean pot. Put the beans in the pot, nest the onion in the center and add the remaining ingredients. Top with remaining half of salt pork. Bake at 300 degrees for 4 to 5 hours. Add water as needed.

Serves 6 to 8.

California Baked Beans

2 cans (32oz. each) **Baked Beans**
4 **Green Peppers**, thinly sliced
4 **Onions**, thinly sliced
6 **Tomatoes**, thinly sliced

1 1/2 tsp. **Salt**
3/4 tsp. freshly **Ground Pepper**
2 tsp. **Sugar**

Preheat oven to 350 degrees.

In a greased casserole, arrange layers of beans, green peppers, and onions and tomatoes. Sprinkle the tomato layers with a mixture of the salt, pepper and sugar. The top layer should be tomato. Bake for 35 minutes.

Beer Batter Fried Veggies 'n' Things

Canola Oil
1 envelope **Lipton® Recipe Secrets® Golden Onion Recipe Soup Mix**
2 cups **All Purpose Flour**
1 tsp. **Baking Powder**
1/2 cup **Beer**
2 **Eggs**
1 tbsp. **Prepared Mustard**

Suggested Veggies 'n' Things

Use any of the following to equal 4 to 5 cups:
Broccoli Florets
Cauliflowerets, Sliced
Mushrooms or **Zucchini**, or
Chilled Mozzarella Sticks

In a deep-fat fryer, heat oil to 375 degrees.

In a large bowl beat soup mix, flour, baking powder, eggs, beer and mustard until smooth and well blended. Let batter stand 10 minutes. Dip suggested veggies into batter and then carefully drop into hot oil. Fry, turning once, until golden brown. Drain on paper towels. Serve warm.

Makes about 4 cups Veggies 'n' Things.

Carrots Vichy

1 bunch **Carrots**
4 tbsp. **Butter**
2 tbsp. **Brown Sugar**
1 tsp. **Parsley Flakes**
1/2 tsp. **Salt**
1/8 tsp. **White Pepper**

Peel carrots and slice into thin rounds. Put in a saucepan with enough water to cover. Add remaining ingredients. Simmer over very low heat, uncovered, until liquid is almost completely evaporated. Make sure that all the carrot rounds are mixed gently to be evenly glazed and lightly browned.

Serves 4 to 6.

Corn Pudding

3 **Eggs**
2 cups **Milk**
2 tbsp. **Sugar**
1 tsp. **Salt**
2 cups **Whole Kernel Corn**, drained
1/4 cup chopped **Green Pepper**
1 chopped **Pimiento**
1 tbsp. melted **Butter**
1 tbsp. minced **Onion**

Preheat oven to 325 degrees.

Beat eggs slightly. Add milk, sugar, and salt. Combine rest of ingredients and add to milk mixture. Turn into greased casserole and bake 1 hour.

Country Hominy Grits

1 cup **Boiling Water**
1 tsp. **Salt**
3/4 cup **Hominy Grits**
2 cups **Milk**

1/4 cup **Butter**
1 tbsp. **Sugar**
1 **Egg**, beaten

Preheat oven to 350 degrees.

Mix water and salt and add hominy grits stirring constantly, until water is absorbed. Add 1 cup milk and cook in top of double boiler one hour. Add butter, sugar, remaining milk and egg and blend thoroughly. Pour in greased casserole and bake one hour.

Serves 4. Serve in place of potatoes.

Never Fail Dumplings

1 **Egg**, beaten
1/2 cup **Milk**
2/3 tsp. **Salt**

1 cup **Flour**
1 tbsp. **Baking Powder**
2 tbsp. **Cornstarch**

Combine egg and milk. Add to remaining dry ingredients. Drop by tablespoonful into boiling stew. Cover and cook 15 minutes. DO NOT PEEK! Cook uncovered 5 minutes.

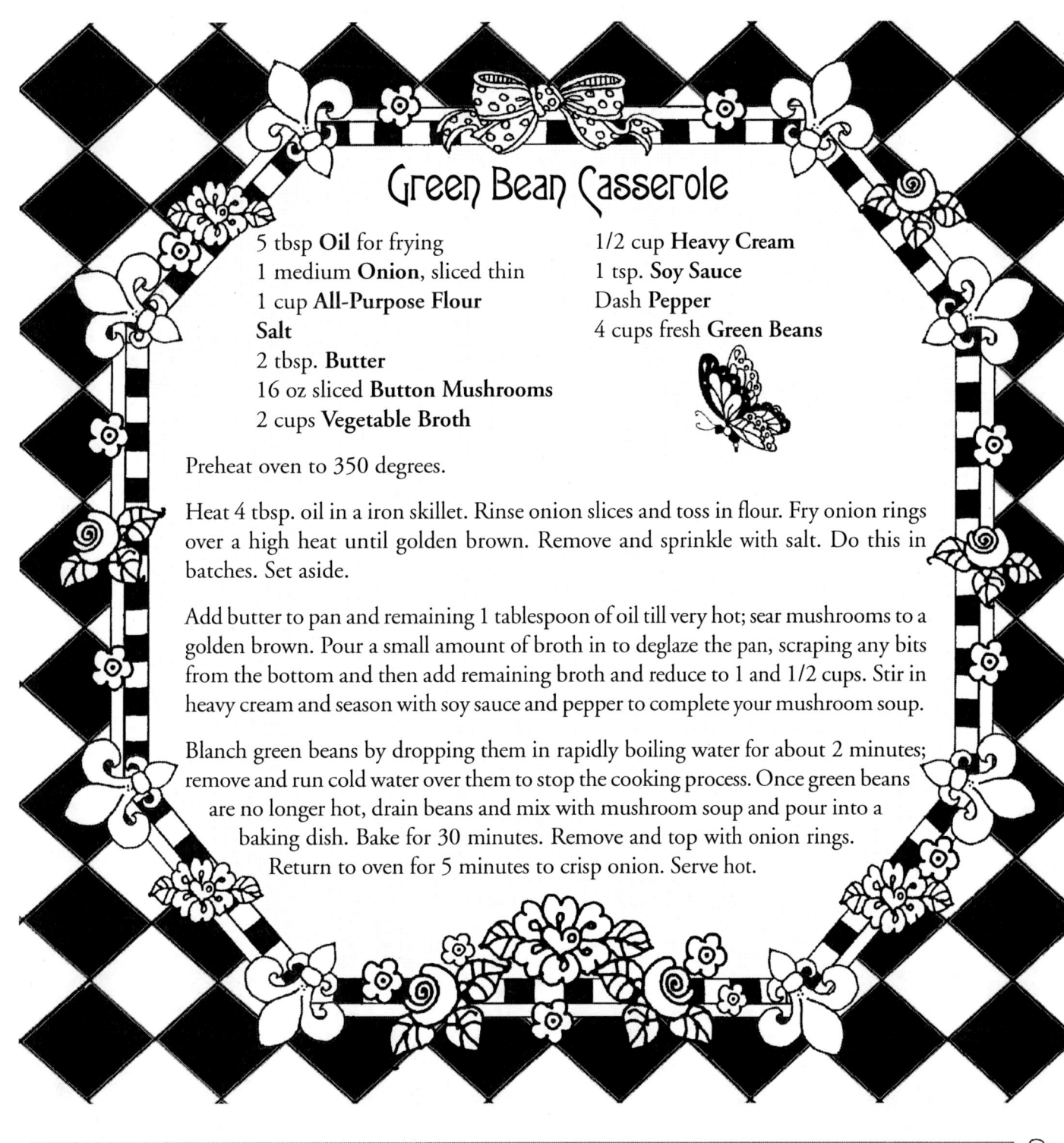

Green Bean Casserole

5 tbsp **Oil** for frying
1 medium **Onion**, sliced thin
1 cup **All-Purpose Flour**
Salt
2 tbsp. **Butter**
16 oz sliced **Button Mushrooms**
2 cups **Vegetable Broth**

1/2 cup **Heavy Cream**
1 tsp. **Soy Sauce**
Dash **Pepper**
4 cups fresh **Green Beans**

Preheat oven to 350 degrees.

Heat 4 tbsp. oil in a iron skillet. Rinse onion slices and toss in flour. Fry onion rings over a high heat until golden brown. Remove and sprinkle with salt. Do this in batches. Set aside.

Add butter to pan and remaining 1 tablespoon of oil till very hot; sear mushrooms to a golden brown. Pour a small amount of broth in to deglaze the pan, scraping any bits from the bottom and then add remaining broth and reduce to 1 and 1/2 cups. Stir in heavy cream and season with soy sauce and pepper to complete your mushroom soup.

Blanch green beans by dropping them in rapidly boiling water for about 2 minutes; remove and run cold water over them to stop the cooking process. Once green beans are no longer hot, drain beans and mix with mushroom soup and pour into a baking dish. Bake for 30 minutes. Remove and top with onion rings. Return to oven for 5 minutes to crisp onion. Serve hot.

Giblet Bread Stuffing

2 lbs. **Poultry Giblets** (ask your supermarket butcher)
2 **Onions**, sliced
2 tsp. **Salt** or to taste
3 to 4 stalks **Celery**
6 cups dry **Bread Crumbs** (18 dry slices)
1/4 tsp. **Pepper**
1 tsp. **Sage**
1 cup **Milk**
2 cups reserved **Broth from Giblets**
2 **Eggs**, beaten slightly

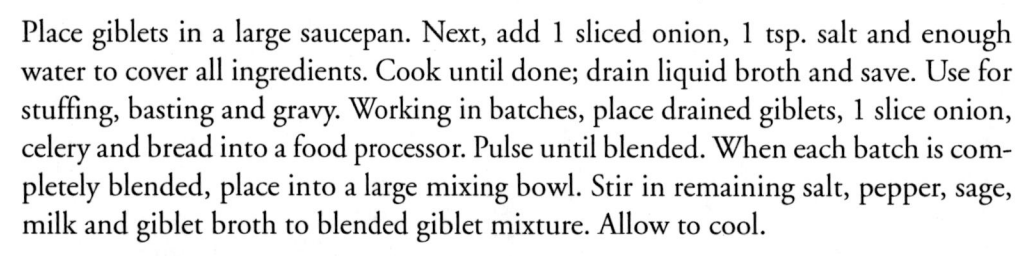

Preheat oven to 350 degrees.

Place giblets in a large saucepan. Next, add 1 sliced onion, 1 tsp. salt and enough water to cover all ingredients. Cook until done; drain liquid broth and save. Use for stuffing, basting and gravy. Working in batches, place drained giblets, 1 slice onion, celery and bread into a food processor. Pulse until blended. When each batch is completely blended, place into a large mixing bowl. Stir in remaining salt, pepper, sage, milk and giblet broth to blended giblet mixture. Allow to cool.

Just before baking, blend in eggs to cooled mixture.

You may prefer more than the 2 cups of broth called for—stuffing should be moist but not soupy.

Makes enough stuffing for 20-25 lb. turkey or bake for 30 minutes in 2 large baking dishes, basting occasionally with giblet broth.

This is a very rich stuffing.

Hush Puppies

2 cups **Corn Meal**
1 tbsp. **Flour**
1/2 tsp. **Baking Soda**
1 tsp. **Baking Powder**
1 tsp. **Salt**
4 tbsp. chopped **Onion**
1 cup **Buttermilk**
1 **Egg**, beaten

Mix all dry ingredients together. Add onion, then milk, then the beaten egg. Drop by spoonful into hot fat. Fry until golden brown.

Noodle and Cheese Kugel

A kugel is a traditional Jewish dish that literally translates to both "ball" and "pudding." There are many variations and some are sweeter than others. This one is served, however, with the meal.

1 package (12 oz.) medium **Noodles**
1 package (4 oz.) **Cream Cheese**
2 **Eggs**, beaten
Sugar and **Cinnamon** to taste
1 cup **Cottage Cheese**
1 grated **Apple**
1 cup **Sour Cream**

Preheat oven to 350 degrees.

Parboil noodles in salt water and drain. Add remaining ingredients and mix thoroughly. Bake in buttered casserole about 45 minutes to 1 hour. Serve hot with sour cream.

Noodle Pudding

1 package (12 oz.) wide **Noodles**
1/2 cup **Raisins** (optional)
1/2 cup **Sugar**
2 **Eggs**, beaten
1/2 tsp. **Vanilla Extract**
1 cup **Milk**
1/2 tsp. **Cinnamon**
4 tbsp. **Butter**

Preheat oven to 350 degrees.

Boil noodles in salted water until tender and drain. Combine with all remaining ingredients and pour into well-greased casserole. Sprinkle with a little more cinnamon if desired. Bake covered 30 minutes. Remove cover and continue baking 30 minutes longer.

This German-inspired dish is best served with some braised meats as an accompaniment, rather than a type of dessert pudding.

Easy Potatoes Au Gratin

1 1/2 lbs. frozen **Hash Brown Potatoes**
1/4 lb. **Butter**
1/2 lb. **American Processed Cheese Spread**
1/2 pint **Half & Half** or **Milk**
4 oz. grated **Sharp Cheddar Cheese**

Preheat oven to 350 degrees.

Arrange frozen hash brown potatoes in a 9 x 9 inch baking dish. Melt all remaining ingredients in a saucepan; pour over potatoes; stir gently to mix. Cover and refrigerate for one hour or longer. Bake uncovered for one hour

Makes 9 to 12 servings.

Shrimp-Stuffed Acorn Squash

2 **Acorn Squash**
1/2 cup **Water**
3 cups **Bread Cubes**
1/4 cup **Butter**
1/4 tsp. **Salt**
1/8 tsp. **Pepper**
1/4 cup chopped **Onions**
1 can (6 oz.) **Shrimp**

Preheat oven to 400 degrees.

Halve acorn squash and remove seeds. Place cut side down in large shallow pan and add 1/2 cup water. Bake at 400 degrees for 20 minutes. While baking, sauté bread cubes in butter. Add salt, pepper, onion, and drained shrimp. Fill cooked squash with stuffing mixture and bake at 350 degrees for 15 to 20 minutes until brown on top.

Baked Hominy

1 can (28 oz.) **Golden Hominy**
1 can (16 oz.) **Stewed Tomatoes**
1/3 lb. shredded **Cheddar Cheese**
2/3 tsp. **Chili Powder**
1 cup sliced **Mushrooms**

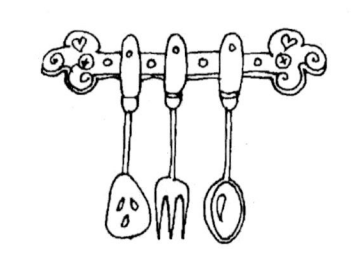

Mix all ingredients in a mixing bowl and pour into a greased baking pan. Bake 30 minutes at 350 degrees. This is delicious served with ham.

Sausage-Zucchini Boats

4 medium **Zucchini** (2 lbs.)
1/4 lb. **Bulk Pork Sausage**
1/4 cup chopped **Onion**
1 large clove fresh **Garlic**, chopped
2 tbsp. **Olive Oil**
1/2 cup **Fine Cracker Crumbs**

1 **Egg**, slightly beaten
1/2 cup grated **Parmesan Cheese**
1/4 tsp. **Salt**
1/4 tsp. **Thyme**
Dash **Paprika**

Preheat oven to 350 degrees.

Steam whole zucchini until barely tender, about 7 minutes. Cut in half lengthwise; scoop squash from shells and mash. Sauté sausage with onion and garlic; drain. Stir in mashed zucchini. Add remaining ingredients (except paprika), reserving 2 tbsp. Parmesan cheese. Mix well; spoon into zucchini shells. Place shells in a shallow baking dish. Sprinkle with reserved Parmesan cheese and dash paprika. Bake 25 to 30 minutes.

Spinach Pie

1 package (4 oz.) **Cream Cheese**, softened
1 cup **Half & Half**
1/2 cup lightly packed soft **Bread Cubes**
1/4 cup shredded **Parmesan Cheese**
2 **Eggs**, slightly beaten
1 cup cooked, very well drained and finely chopped **Fresh Spinach**, about 1 1/4 lbs.
4 tbsp. **Butter**
1 large **Onion**, finely chopped
1/2 lb. **Mushrooms**, finely chopped
1 tsp. **Tarragon**
3/4 tsp. **Salt** (approximately)
1 unbaked (9-inch) **Pie Shell**

Preheat oven to 400 degrees.

Mash cream cheese with fork, and gradually blend in half & half. Add bread cubes, Parmesan cheese, and eggs to cream cheese. Mix and beat with rotary mixer or wire whip to break up bread pieces. Stir in spinach. Melt butter in wide frying pan; cook onion and mushrooms until lightly browned, stirring frequently; add tarragon when vegetables are soft. Blend hot vegetables with spinach mix. Salt to taste. Pour vegetable filling into pastry shell. Bake on lowest rack in hot oven for 25 minutes or until crust is well browned. Let stand 10 minutes before cutting. Serve hot or cold. Makes 6 to 8 servings.

Spinach Parmesan

    3 lbs. **Spinach**, cleaned thoroughly
    6 tbsp. **Parmesan Cheese**
    6 tbsp. minced **Onion**
    6 tbsp. **Heavy Cream**
    5 tbsp. melted **Butter**
    1/2 cup **Cracker Crumbs**

Preheat oven to 350 degrees.

Cook the cleaned spinach until just starting to wilt (will cook very fast). Drain thoroughly. Chop coarsely and add the cheese, onion, cream and 4 tbsp. butter. Arrange in a shallow baking dish and sprinkle with the crumbs mixed with the remaining butter. Bake for 10 to 15 minutes.

Succotash

    2 cups cooked **Lima Beans**
    2 tbsp. **Butter**
    2 cups cooked **Corn**
    1/2 cup **Heavy Cream**
    1/2 tsp. **Salt**
    Pepper to taste

Combine beans and corn. Add seasonings, butter and cream. Heat and serve at once. Serves 6 to 8.

Sweet Potato Casserole

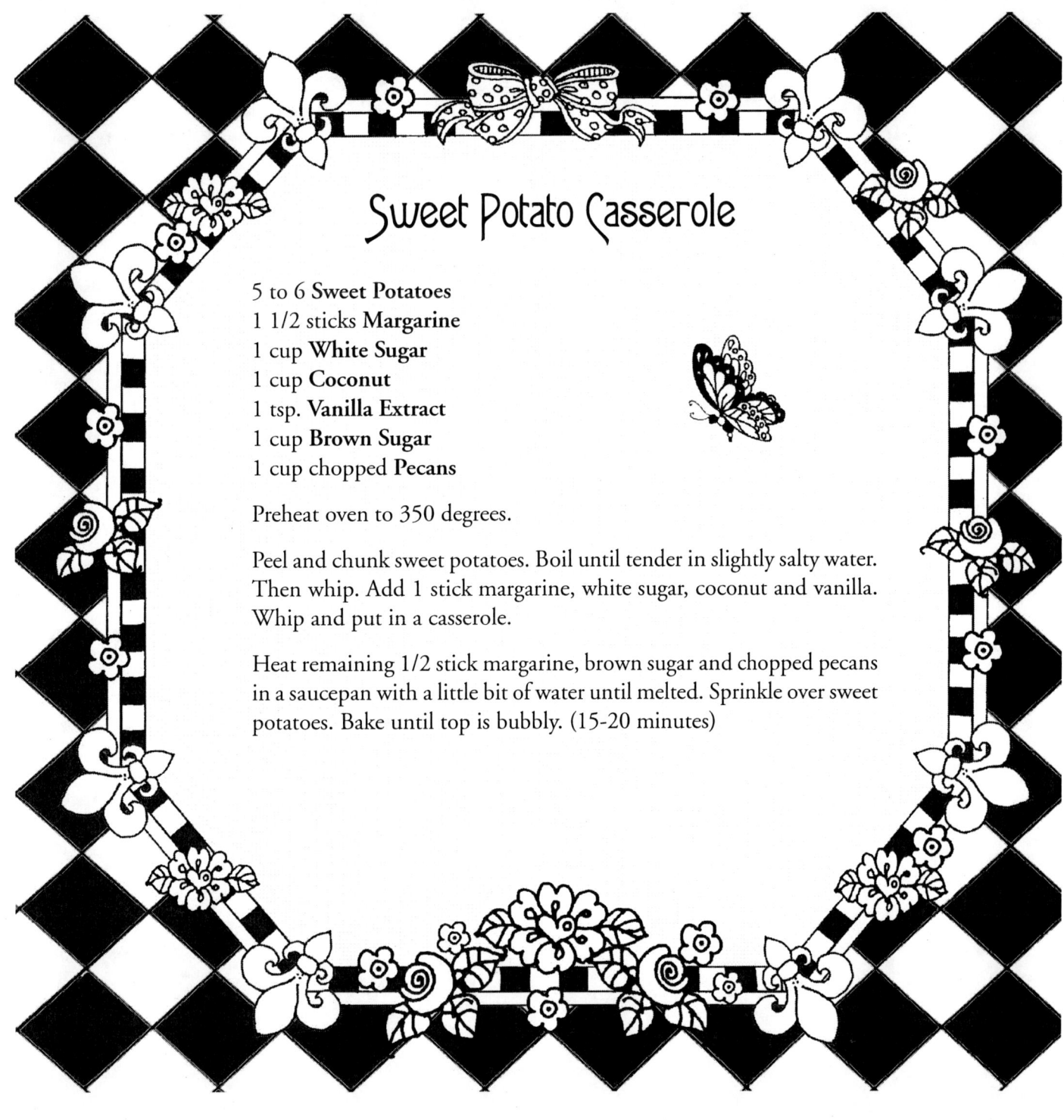

5 to 6 **Sweet Potatoes**
1 1/2 sticks **Margarine**
1 cup **White Sugar**
1 cup **Coconut**
1 tsp. **Vanilla Extract**
1 cup **Brown Sugar**
1 cup chopped **Pecans**

Preheat oven to 350 degrees.

Peel and chunk sweet potatoes. Boil until tender in slightly salty water. Then whip. Add 1 stick margarine, white sugar, coconut and vanilla. Whip and put in a casserole.

Heat remaining 1/2 stick margarine, brown sugar and chopped pecans in a saucepan with a little bit of water until melted. Sprinkle over sweet potatoes. Bake until top is bubbly. (15-20 minutes)

Easy Wild Rice-Mushroom Stuffing

1 package (6 oz.) **Long Grain and Wild Rice Mix**
2 tbsp. **Butter** or **Margarine**
2 tbsp. chopped **Onion**
1 can (4 oz.) **Mushrooms Stems and Pieces**
1 tbsp. chopped **Parsley**

Cook rice mix according to package directions. Melt butter or margarine in a small skillet; cook onions until soft. Drain and chop mushrooms. Combine cooked wild rice mixture, onion, mushrooms, and parsley. Mix well. Stuff lightly into neck cavity of 16 to 18 lbs. turkey.

You have to be very careful when cooking stuffing or dressing inside of the cavity of poultry. Even if your bird reaches its internal temperature of 165 F, you MUST make sure the stuffing does, as well. The juices from the bird drip all throughout your dressing and if the temperature doesn't reach its proper level, you risk the same salmonella bacteria of an undercooked bird. Just be cautious.

DESSERTS

Dessert, upon translation, essentially means to "clear the table." The first desserts were thought to be an assortment of fruits—which were essential in the aiding of digestion. This is particularly true in Asia and is thought to have spread about the world. The wealthy, of course, took this concept to new heights and absurdity until the dessert table had just as much food on it as the rest of the meal. Over the centuries and over cultures it has morphed into what we have today, which is some sort of basic sweet course that ends the meal. Almost every household today highlights special occasions with a sweet treat. Grandma is adored for her baking, but even she had her limit as to how much "junk" was allowed into our bodies. For those special occasions we all enjoy, Grandma has provided us with the following recipes.

Desserts

Amazin' Raisin Cake	141
Nana's Fudge Cake	142
Peach Cobbler	142
Sunday Special Coffee Cake	143
Zucchini Cake	144
Never Fail Fudge	144
Grandma's Chocolate Chip Cookies	145
The Best Oatmeal Cookies	146
Peanut Butter Cookies	146
Apple Pie in a Paper Bag	147
Flaky Pie Crusts	148
Pumpkin Pie Filling	148

Amazin' Raisin Cake

3 cups **Flour**
2 cups **Sugar**
1 cup **Mayonnaise**
1/3 cup **Milk**
2 **Eggs**
2 tsp. **Baking Soda**
1 1/2 tsp. **Ground Cinnamon**
1/2 tsp. **Nutmeg**
1/2 tsp. **Salt**
1/4 tsp. **Ground Cloves**
3 cups peeled and chopped **Apples**
1 cup **Seedless Raisins**
1/2 cup chopped **Walnuts**
2 cups **Whipped Cream**

Preheat oven to 350 degrees.

Grease and flour two cake pans. In large bowl with mixer at low speed, beat the first ten ingredients 2 minutes. Stir in apples, raisins and nuts. Pour into pans and bake for 45 minutes or until done. Cool in pans for 10 minutes. Remove from pan and let cool. Frost with whipped cream.

Nana's Fudge Cake

3 oz. **Unsweetened Chocolate**
1/2 cup **Butter**
2 1/4 cups lightly packed **Light Brown Sugar**
3 **Eggs**
1 1/2 tsp. **Vanilla Extract**

2 tsp. **Baking Soda**
1/2 tsp. **Salt**
2 1/4 cups **Flour**
1 cup **Sour Cream**
1 cup **Boiling Water**

Preheat oven to 350 degrees.

Grease two cake pans. Melt chocolate, set aside. In large mixing bowl, cream butter until smooth. Add brown sugar and eggs. Beat with mixer on high speed until light and fluffy, about 5 minutes. With mixer on low speed, beat in the vanilla, melted chocolate, soda and salt. Add flour alternately with sour cream, beating on low until smooth. Pour in boiling water, stir with spoon until blended. Then pour into cake pans. Bake 35 minutes or until done. Cool in pans. Turn on wire racks to cool completely. Frost if desired.

Peach Cobbler

1 1/2 cups **Sugar**, divided
1 cup **Flour**
1 tsp. **Baking Powder**
1/4 tsp. **Salt**

6 tbsp. melted **Margarine**, divided
1/2 cup **Milk**
1 can (8 oz.) **Sliced Peaches**

Preheat oven to 375 degrees.

Mix together 1 cup sugar, flour, baking powder and salt. In another bowl, stir 3 tablespoons margarine and milk until creamy. Mix together. Butter a 9 x 13 pan and pour in batter. Add the sliced peaches. Sprinkle 1/2 cup sugar on top and pour 3 tablespoons margarine. Place in oven for 40 to 60 minutes.

Sunday Special Coffee Cake

Topping:
1/2 cup **Sugar**
1/4 cup sifted **Flour**
1/4 cup **Butter**, softened
1 tsp. **Cinnamon**

Preheat oven to 375 degrees.

Grease an 8 x 8 x 2 inch baking dish. In small bowl, combine sugar, flour, butter and cinnamon. Mix lightly with fork, until crumbly, set aside.

Batter:

1 1/2 cups sifted **Flour**	3/4 cup **Sugar**
2 1/2 tsp. **Baking Powder**	1/3 cup melted **Butter**
1/2 tsp. **Salt**	1/2 cup **Milk**
1 **Egg**	1 tsp. **Vanilla Extract**

Sift flour with baking powder and salt, set aside. In a medium bowl, beat egg until frothy then beat in sugar and melted butter until well combined. Add milk and vanilla. With wooden spoon, beat in flour mixture until well combined. Pour into prepared pan. Sprinkle topping evenly over batter. Bake 25-30 minutes. Cool partially, in pan. Cut into squares while still warm. Makes 9 servings.

Desserts 143

Zucchini Cake

3 **Eggs**	1/2 tsp. **Ground Nutmeg**
2 cups **Sugar**	1 tsp. **Ground Cinnamon**
1 cup **Vegetable Oil**	1/8 tsp. **Allspice**
1 tsp. **Salt**	2 cups shredded **Zucchini**
1 tsp. **Baking Powder**	1/4 cup **Milk**
1 tsp. **Baking Soda**	3 cups **Flour**
1 tsp. **Vanilla Extract**	1 cup chopped **Walnuts**

Preheat oven to 350 degrees.

Grease and flour bundt pan. Mix together eggs, sugar, oil, salt, baking powder, baking soda, vanilla, nutmeg, cinnamon and allspice and beat on low speed for one minute. Add zucchini and milk and blend together. Gradually add the flour and beat at medium speed until smooth. Stir in the walnuts and pour into pan. Bake for 1 hour and 10 minutes. Cool in pan for 15 minutes, then on wire rack until completely cool.

Never Fail Fudge

1 can (12 oz.) **Evaporated Milk**	1/4 lb. **Butter** or **Margarine**
4 cups **Sugar**	1 package (12 oz.) **Semi-Sweet Chocolate Chips**
1 pint **Marshmallow Crème** or	
3 cups **Small Marshmallows**	

Place milk, butter or margarine, and sugar in saucepan and cook until it forms a soft ball (230 F.), about 6 minutes. Stir often to keep from burning. Remove from heat and fold in the semi-sweet chocolate chips and the marshmallows. Pour into a greased 9 x 12 dish. Cool. Place in the refrigerator.

144   *Grandma's Favorite Country Recipes*

Grandma's Chocolate Chip Cookies

2 cups **Butter**
2 cups **Granulated Sugar**
2 cups **Brown Sugar**
4 **Eggs**
2 tsp. **Vanilla Extract**
5 cups **Oatmeal**
4 cups **Flour**
1 tsp. **Salt**
2 tsp. **Baking Powder**
2 tsp. **Baking Soda**
2 packages (12 oz.) **Semi-Sweet Chocolate Chips**
1 **Hershey® Bar** (8 oz.) grated
3 cups chopped **Nuts**

Preheat oven to 350 degrees.

Cream together butter, granulated sugar, and brown sugar. Add eggs and vanilla to butter-sugar mixture. Put 1/2 cup of oatmeal in a blender and blend until it is a powder. In a separate bowl, mix together the flour, oatmeal (including the oatmeal that was treated in the blender), salt, baking powder, and baking soda. Mix together all ingredients, adding chocolate chips, Hershey bar and nuts. Drop dough by rounded tablespoons onto ungreased cookie sheet, 2 inches apart. Bake about 10 to 15 minutes, or until slightly golden.

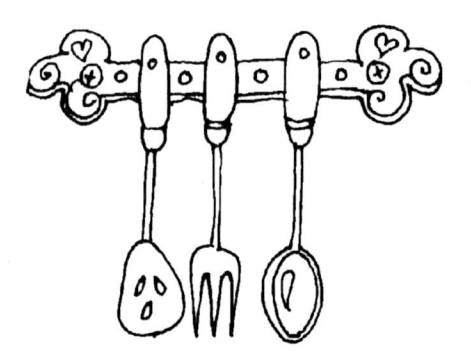

The "Best" Oatmeal Cookies

2 **Eggs**, well beaten
1 cup **Raisins**
1 tsp. **Vanilla Extract**
1 cup **Butter**
1 cup **Brown Sugar**
1 cup **White Sugar**
2 1/2 cups **Flour**
1 tsp. **Salt**
1 tsp. **Ground Cinnamon**
2 tsp. **Baking Soda**
2 cups **Oatmeal**
3/4 cup chopped **Pecans**

Preheat oven to 350 degrees.

Combine eggs, raisins and vanilla and let stand for one hour, covered with plastic wrap. Cream together butter and sugars. Add flour, salt, cinnamon and soda to sugar mixture. Mix well. Blend in egg-raisin mixture, oatmeal and chopped nuts. Dough will be very stiff. Drop by heaping teaspoons onto ungreased cookie sheet, or roll into small balls and flatten slightly on cookie sheet. Bake for 10 to 12 minutes or until lightly browned.

Note: Secret is soaking of the raisins.

Peanut Butter Cookies

1 cup **Shortening**
1 cup **Peanut Butter**
1 cup **Granulated Sugar**
1 cup packed **Brown Sugar**
2 **Eggs**
1 tsp. **Vanilla Extract**
2 1/2 cups **Flour**
1/2 tsp. **Salt**
3/4 tsp. **Baking Soda**
1/2 tsp. **Baking Powder**

Preheat oven to 375 degrees.

Beat shortening and peanut butter until creamy. Gradually add sugars, beating thoroughly after each addition. Beat in eggs and vanilla. Mix remaining ingredients and blend into peanut butter mixture. Shape dough into balls about 1" in diameter. Place 2" apart on ungreased baking sheet. Flatten each cookie. Crisscross top of each cookie with a fork. Bake for 10 to 15 minutes. Remove from baking sheet while warm.

Apple Pie in a Paper Bag

3 or 4 large **Baking Apples** (about 2 1/2 lbs.)
1/2 cup **Sugar** (for filling)
1/4 cup **Flour** (for filling)
1/2 tsp. **Nutmeg**
1/2 tsp. **Cinnamon**
2 tbsp. **Lemon Juice**
1/2 cup **Sugar**
1/2 cup **Butter** or **Margarine**
1/2 cup **Flour** (for topping)
1 unbaked (9-inch) **Pie Shell**

Preheat oven to 425 degrees.

Pare, core and slice apples. Place in large bowl. Combine sugar, flour and spices in bowl for filling and then sprinkle over apples. Toss to coat well and spoon into pastry shell. Drizzle with lemon juice. Combine remaining sugar and flour in small bowl. Cut in butter or margarine and sprinkle over apples, covering top. Slide pie into heavy brown paper bag, large enough to cover pie loosely. Fold open end over twice and fasten with paper clips. Place on cookie sheet for easier handling. Bake for 1 hour. Split bag open, remove pie and serve.

It is delicious warm, with ice cream. This is good for any fruit pie and when done it is a golden brown. Never fails.

Flaky Pie Crust

4 cups **Flour**
2 tsp. **Salt**
1 tsp. **Baking Powder**
1 1/2 cups **Shortening**

1 **Egg**
1 tbsp. **Vinegar**
1/2 cup **Cold Water**

Sift together flour, salt and baking powder. Cut in shortening. Beat egg. Add vinegar and water to it. Gradually add liquid to flour mixture and combine. Add a little more water if needed. Divide dough into quarters. Wrap in wax paper and refrigerate until ready to use.

Pumpkin Pie Filling—Fresh

1 medium **Pumpkin**
1/2 tsp. **Salt**
1 1/2 cups **Sugar**
1 tsp. (heaping) **Cinnamon**
1 tsp. **Allspice** or **Pumpkin Pie Spice**
3 **Eggs**
3 1/2 cups **Milk**

Preheat oven to 425 degrees.

Peel pumpkin and dice; you should get 3 cups. Boil with salt and enough water to cover for about 1/2 hour until pumpkin is soft. Strain and mash immediately. Add sugar, cinnamon and allspice. Blend in well-beaten eggs and milk. Pour mixture into 2 unbaked pie shells and bake at least 45 minutes.

BEVERAGES

A drink that requires several ingredients to qualify as a recipe is more commonly known as punch. Punch is thought, for the most part, to root its history from India where the word itself—panch—means five. This most likely is referring to the typical five ingredients necessary to make it. Different regions had different elements, but for the most part they all contained alcohol to some degree. These days punch has so many variations that the list is practically endless.

Beverages

Cranberry Punch 151
Dandelion Wine 151
Gala Holiday Punch 152
Holiday Punch 152
Hot Apple Cider 153
Pineapple Lemonade 153
Peach-Berry Punch 154
Root Beer—Home Brewed 155
Sangria 155
Orange Slush 156
Wine Cooler Punch 156

Cranberry Punch

1/2 cup **Sugar**
1 1/2 cups **Water**
1 can (12 oz.) frozen **Orange Juice Concentrate**

2 pints **Cranberry Juice**
4 tbsp. **Lemon Juice**
7-Up® as needed

Simmer water and sugar together until sugar is dissolved, 3 to 5 minutes and cool. Combine all ingredients in punch bowl and mix. Add equal part of punch and 7-Up.

This recipe is certainly one of the most unique that has come across Grandma's counter. Home brewing and wine making is certainly an art from the past, nevertheless its process is simple. The biggest ingredient is patience!

Dandelion Wine

5 quarts **Dandelion Blossoms**
8 quarts **Water**
Juice of 1 **Orange** and 1 **Lemon**
1 cup **Raisins**
3 lbs. **Sugar**
1/2 **Yeast Cake**
5 months of patience

Pick 5 quarts of dandelion blossoms. Boil for 1 1/2 hours in 8 quarts of water.

For 1 gallon of wine, use 4 quarts of dandelion juice and juice of 1 orange and 1 lemon. Strain dandelion, orange and lemon juice. Boil raisins and strain (do not use raisin seeds or pulp). Put ingredients in a crock jar. Add 1/2 yeast cake last. Mix well.

Use a cloth under the cover of the jar. Allow fermentation for 5 months before bottling.

Gala Holiday Punch

4 medium **Grapefruit**, peeled and cut-up
1 bottle (67.6 oz.) **Lemon-Lime Soda**
1/4 cup **Sugar**, optional
1 pint **Lime Sherbet**
1 pint **Pineapple Sherbet**

In a food processor purée the cut-up grapefruit until nearly smooth. Strain into a large bowl, squeezing out every last drop. Discard pulp. Add 1 quart of the lemon-lime soda to the grapefruit juice. Stir in sugar till dissolved. Pour into a 9 x 9 x 2 inch pan. Cover and freeze 4 to 5 hours or until nearly firm, stirring three times. At serving time, spoon sherbet into punch bowl. Spoon grapefruit mixture into punch bowl. Pour in remaining carbonated beverage. Makes 1 gallon.

Holiday Punch

1 bottle **Champagne**, chilled
2 bottles (1 quart each) **Ginger Ale**, chilled
1 1/4 cups **Cranberry Juice**
1/4 cup **Raspberry Syrup**
2 **Oranges**, sliced (optional)
2 **Limes**, sliced (optional)
1 bag (12 oz.) frozen **Raspberries** (optional)

Combine champagne, ginger ale, cranberry juice and raspberry syrup in punch bowl. Add oranges, limes and raspberries.

Hot Apple Cider

2 tsp. **Cloves**
2 sticks **Cinnamon**
2 tsp. whole **Allspice Berries**
2/3 cup **Sugar**
1 gallon **Cider**
1 **Orange**, sliced

Combine all ingredients and bring to a boil. Simmer 20 minutes. Strain and serve warm.

Option 2:

Place all ingredients in a slow cooker and heat on low for 6 hours. Strain out whole spices and serve right from cooker.

Pineapple Lemonade

1 pint **Water**
1 cup **Sugar**
1 can (8 oz.) **Crushed Pineapple**
Juice of 3 **Lemons**
1 quart **Ice Water**

Make syrup by boiling water and sugar 10 minutes. Take off of heat and add pineapple and lemon juice. Cool, strain and add ice water.

A scrumptious drink.

Peach-Berry Punch

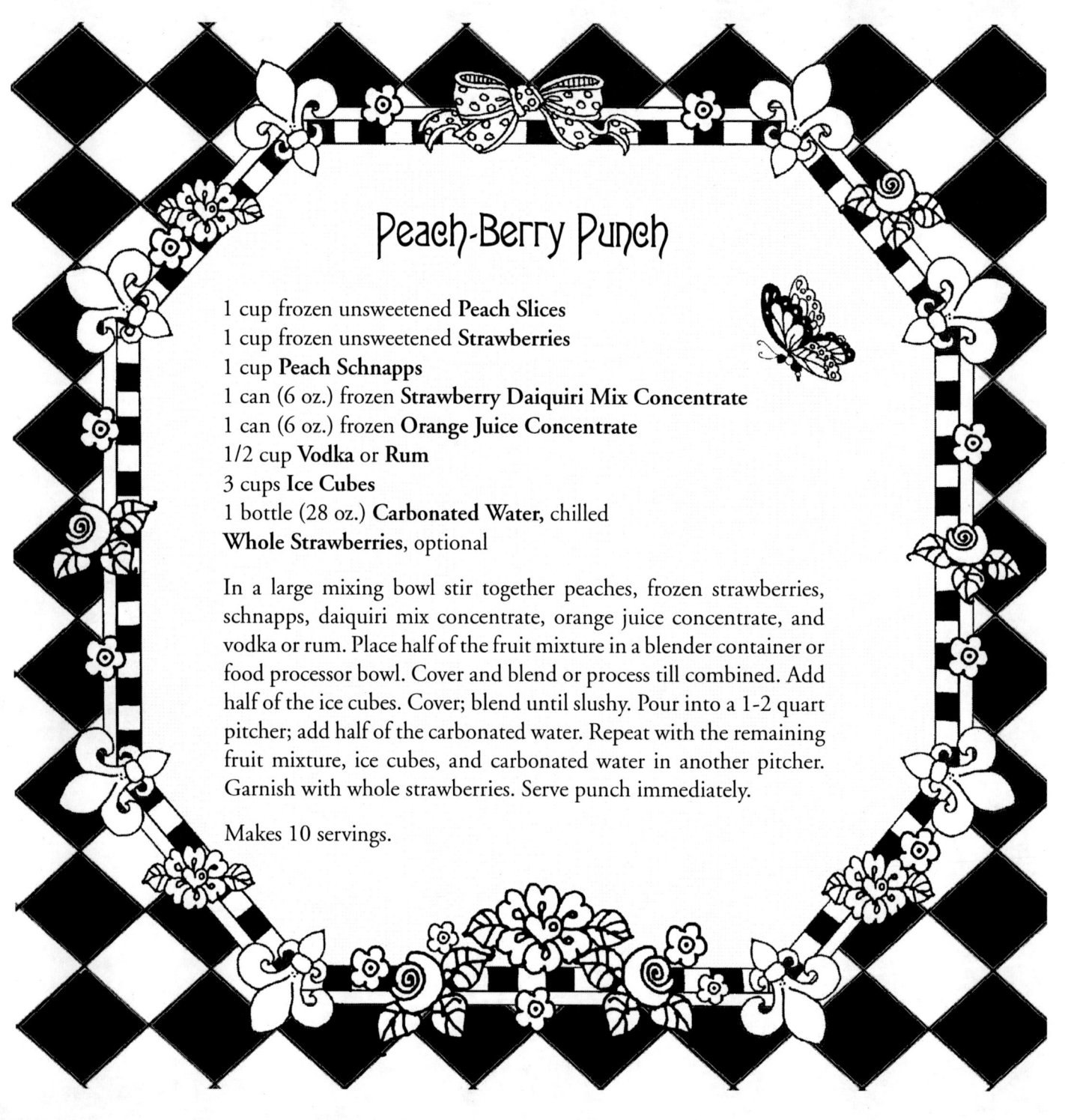

1 cup frozen unsweetened **Peach Slices**
1 cup frozen unsweetened **Strawberries**
1 cup **Peach Schnapps**
1 can (6 oz.) frozen **Strawberry Daiquiri Mix Concentrate**
1 can (6 oz.) frozen **Orange Juice Concentrate**
1/2 cup **Vodka** or **Rum**
3 cups **Ice Cubes**
1 bottle (28 oz.) **Carbonated Water**, chilled
Whole Strawberries, optional

In a large mixing bowl stir together peaches, frozen strawberries, schnapps, daiquiri mix concentrate, orange juice concentrate, and vodka or rum. Place half of the fruit mixture in a blender container or food processor bowl. Cover and blend or process till combined. Add half of the ice cubes. Cover; blend until slushy. Pour into a 1-2 quart pitcher; add half of the carbonated water. Repeat with the remaining fruit mixture, ice cubes, and carbonated water in another pitcher. Garnish with whole strawberries. Serve punch immediately.

Makes 10 servings.

Root Beer—Home Brewed

A non-alcoholic carbonated drink to enjoy.

4 lbs. **Sugar**
4 3/4 gallons **Lukewarm Water**
1 bottle (2 oz.) **Root Beer Extract**
1/2 tsp. **Fleishmann's® Dried Yeast** or 1/2 cake of **Fleishmann's® Yeast**
 dissolved in 1 cup lukewarm water.

Dissolve sugar in 4 3/4 gallon lukewarm water; add Root Beer extract then dissolved yeast. Stir well and bottle immediately, fastening the cork in securely or seal with crown caps. Fill bottles to within ½ inch of the top—more air space may cause spoilage. Place bottles on their sides in a warm place away from drafts until they become effervescent. Should be ready to drink in 5 days. Then set bottles in a cool place of even temperature.

Sangria

1 **Orange**
1 **Lemon**
1 jigger (1 1/2 oz.) **Cointreau**
1/4 cup **Sugar**
1 bottle (750ml) **Red Wine**
1 or 2 cans **7-Up®**, or to taste
Ice

Slice orange and lemon; add Cointreau, sugar and wine. Stir. Let stand at room temperature 1 to 2 hours. Just before serving add 7-Up® and serve iced.

Beverages 155

Orange Slush

1 can (12 oz.) frozen **Orange Juice Concentrate**, mix as directed
1 package **Cherry Kool-Aid**®
1 can (12 oz.) frozen **Lemonade Concentrate**, mix as directed
1 can (12 oz.) **Ginger Ale**
1 can (46 oz.) **Unsweetened Pineapple Juice**
16 oz. **Vodka**
2 1/2 cups **Sugar**
7-Up®

Mix all ingredients except 7-Up® and freeze. To serve, scrape slush into glasses and cover with 7-Up®.

Wine Cooler Punch

1/2 cup **Water**
1/2 cup **Sugar**
1 can (6 oz.) **Lemonade Concentrate**
1 Fifth **Chablis**, chilled
1 Fifth **Ginger Ale**, chilled

Combine water and sugar in small saucepan. Bring sugar water to a boil and let cool completely. When cool add 6 oz. can of lemonade concentrate. Add chablis and ginger ale. Serve immediately. Makes 20 servings, about 1/2 cup each.

Index

A
Amazin' Raisin Cake 141
America's Meat Loaf With Cheese Stuffing 109
Angel Or Devil Breakfast Casserole 22
Appetizers 76
   Artichoke Dip, Hot 77
   Bacon Roll-Ups 78
   Bourbon Hot Dogs 78
   Cheese Ball 83
   Chicken Liver Paté 79
   Deviled Eggs 80
   Dilly Dip 80
   Krazy Meatballs 81
   Stuffed Mushrooms 81
   Sweet and Sour Meatballs 82-83
   Tex-Mex Dip 84
Apple Muffins 53
Apple Pie in a Paper Bag 147
Artichoke Dip—Hot 77
Aunt Amy Earhart's Banana Nut Bread 54
Aunt Kate's Blueberry Muffins 55

B
Bacon Roll-Ups 78
Baked Asparagus 123
Baked Hominy 134
Banana Sticky Buns 56
Barbequed Beef 87
Barbequed Chicken 88
Barbequed Spare Ribs 89
Bean and Red Cabbage Salad 32
Beans 31-32, 36, 49, 90, 124, 136
Beef Stroganoff 95
Beef-Bean-Herb Casserole 90
Beer 56
Beer Batter Fried Veggies 'n' Things 126
Beer Bread 56
"Before There Were Crockpots" Chicken and Rice 103
Beverages 150-151, 153, 155
   Cranberry Punch 151
   Dandelion Wine 151
   Gala Holiday Punch 152
   Holiday Punch 152
   Hot Apple Cider 153
   Orange Slush 156
   Peach-Berry Punch 154
   Pineapple Lemonade 153
   Root Beer 155
   Sangria 155
   Wine Cooler Punch 156
Biscuits—Buttermilk 57
Biscuits—Old Fashioned 57
Boston Baked Beans 125
Bourbon Hot Dogs 78
Bran Muffins 58
Breads/Muffins 52-53, 55, 57, 59, 61, 63, 65, 67, 69, 71, 73
   Apple Muffins 53
   Aunt Amy Earhart's Banana Nut Bread 54
   Aunt Kate's Blueberry Muffins 55
   Banana Sticky Buns 56
   Beer Bread 56
   Biscuits, Buttermilk 57
   Biscuits, Old Fashioned 57
   Bran Muffins 58
   Buttermilk Donuts 59
   Cherry Pecan Bread 59
   Chocolate Cinnamon Muffins 60
   Crusty Biscuits 61
   Date-Nut Pumpkin Bread 62
   Dilly Bread 63
   Gingerbread 64
   Gingerbread Cupcakes 65
   Herb Sour Cream Bread 67
   Hush Puppies 68
   Johnny Cake 66
   Pear Bread 70
   Prune Bread 69
   Pumpkin Bread 70
   Pumpkin Muffins 71-72
   Quick Raisin Bread 72
   Sassy Cinnamon Pecan Muffins 73
   Squash Muffins 73
   Texas Cornbread 74
   Zucchini Nut Bread 74
Breakfasts 9
   Angel or Devil Breakfast Casserole 22
   Chatanooga Corn Fritters 12
   Classic French Toast 15
   Farmland Pancakes 18
   Homemade Waffles 28
   Mean Egg and Cheese Bake 14
   Old Fashioned Pancakes 17
   Perfect Potato Pancakes 19
   Popovers 23
   Quiche 25
   Raised Buckwheat Pancakes 20
   Rice Pancakes 21
   Rich Man Poor Man Crepes 13
   Southern Cornpone 24
   Spinach Quiche 27
   Stuffed French Toast 16
   Sunday Quiche 26
   Traditional Cheese Grits 11
   Zucchini Pancakes 21
Buttermilk Donuts 59

C
Cabbage Slaw 32
California Baked Beans 125
Carrot Salad 33
Carrots Vichy 127
Chatanooga Corn Fritters 12
Cheese 11, 14, 21-22, 25-27, 37, 48, 74, 77-78, 81, 83-84, 90, 93, 96, 100, 106-110, 118, 123, 126, 131, 133-136
Cheese Ball 83
Cherry-Pecan Bread 59
Chicken And Lima Bean Stew 99
Chicken Breasts In Parmesan Cream 93
Chicken Liver Paté 79
Chicken Paprikash 100
Chicken Pie With Crust 101
Chicken Salad 33
Chicken—Herb Roasted 98
Chocolate 144-145
Chocolate Cinnamon Muffins 60
Classic (and Classy) French Toast 15
Classic Chicken Noodle Dish 100
Cocoa 60
Corn Chowder 44
Corn Pudding 127
Country Hominy Grits 128
Cranberry Punch 151
Cream of Wild Rice Soup 45
Crusty Biscuits 61

D
Dairy 35-37, 44-45, 50, 57, 59, 63-65, 67-68, 74, 77, 79-80, 84, 93, 95, 97, 100-105, 114, 129, 131, 133, 135-136, 141-142
Dandelion Wine 151
Date-Nut Pumpkin Bread 62
Desserts 140-141, 143, 145, 147
   Amazin' Raisin Cake 141
   Apple Pie, Paper Bag 147
   Grandma's Chocolate Chip Cookies 145
   Nana's Fudge Cake 142
   Never Fail Fudge 144
   Peach Cobbler 142
   Peanut Butter Cookies 146
   Pie Crust 148
   Pumpkin Pie Filling 148
   Sunday Special Coffee Cake 143
   The "Best" Oatmeal Cookies 146
   Zucchini Cake 144
Deviled Eggs 80
Dilly Bread 63
Dilly Dip 80

E

Easy Burgundy Stew 119
Easy Potatoes Au Gratin 133
Easy Wild Rice-Mushroom Stuffing 138
Eggs 12-17, 22-23, 25-28, 39, 48, 74, 79-80, 100, 109, 123
Elegant Chicken Pilaf Soup 102
Elegant Pilaf 102

F

Farmland Pancakes 18
Fried Chicken In Sour Cream-Sherry Sauce 104
Fruit Salad Deluxe 35
Fruits
    Apples 35, 53, 96, 102, 105, 110, 114, 131, 141, 147
    Bananas 35, 54, 56
    Blueberries 55
    Cherries 35, 59
    Grapefruit 152
    Grapes 35-36
    Lemons 88, 151, 153, 155
    Limes 152
    Oranges 35-36, 151-153, 155
    Peaches 142, 154
    Pears 70
    Pineapple 35
    Pineapples 153
    Prunes 69
    Raisins 62, 71-72, 96, 105, 132, 141, 146, 151
    Raspberries 152
    Strawberries 154

G

Gala Holiday Punch 152
German Potato Salad 38
Giblet Bread Stuffing 130
Gingerbread 64
Gingerbread Cupcakes 65
Glorified Hash 106
Grandma's Chocolate Chip Cookies 145
"Grandma Has A Sore Back" Chicken-N-Rice 103
Green Bean Casserole 129

H

Ham Steak Shuffle 105
Herb Sour Cream Bread 67
Hobo Soup 49
Holiday Punch 152
Home Made Waffles 28
Hot Apple Cider 153
Hot German Potato Salad 39
Hush Puppies 68, 131

J

Johnny Cake 66

K

Krazy Meatballs 81

L

Lasagna—Vegetable 108
Leftover Turkey Salad 36
Liquor
    Beer 126
    Champagne 152
    Cointreau 155
    Rum 154
    Schnapps 154
    Tequila 120
    Vodka 154, 156

M

Macaroni Salad 37
Main Dishes 86-87, 89, 91, 93, 95, 97, 99, 101, 103, 105, 107, 109, 111, 113, 115, 117, 119
    America's Meat Loaf with Cheese Stuffing 109
    Barbequed Beef 87
    Barbequed Chicken 88
    Barbequed Spare Ribs 89
    Beef Stroganoff 95
    Beef-Bean-Herb Casserole 90
    Chicken and Lima Bean Stew 99
    Chicken and Rice 103
    Chicken Breasts in Parmesan Cream 93
    Chicken Paprikash 100
    Chicken Pie with Crust 101
    Chicken, Herb Roasted 98
    Classic Chicken Noodle Dish 100
    Easy Burgundy Stew 119
    Elegant Chicken Pilaf Soup 102
    Fried Chicken in Sour Cream Sherry Sauce 104
    Glorified Hash 106
    Ham Steak Shuffle 105
    Mama's Lasagna 107
    Meat Loaf 110
    Meat Loaf, Apple 110
    Mel's Diner Pork Chop Casserole 112
    Nana's Nuked Chicken and Dumplings 94
    New England Pot Roast 115
    Old Time Beef Stew 91
    Oven Beef Stew 92
    Pork Chop Dinner 115
    Pork Chops, Savory 112
    Pot Roast with Dumplings 116
    Pot Roast with Golden Potatoes 117
    Savory Beef Stew 93
    Shepherd's Pie 118
    Simple Sweet and Sour Pork 120
    Southern Mother's Chicken Fried Steak 97
    Stuffed Cabbage Rolls 118
    Stuffed Chicken Breasts 96
    Stuffed Pork Chops 113
    Stuffed Pork Tenderloin 114
    Tequila Chicken 120
    The "Other White Meat" Loaf 106
    Uptown Manhattan Meat Loaf 111
    Vegetable Lasagna 108
    Walk the Flank Steak 105
Mama's Lasagna 107
Mean Egg and Cheese Bake 14
Meat
    Bacon 37-39, 78, 124
    Beef 87, 90-93, 95, 97, 105, 109-111, 115-117, 119
    Bones 49
    Corned Beef 106
    Ground Beef 46, 81-83, 107, 110, 118
    Ham 26, 105
    Hot Dogs 78
    Leftovers 48
    Pork 89, 106, 112-115, 117, 120
    Sausage 26, 47, 134
    Turkey 36
Meat Loaf 110
Meat Loaf—Apple 110
Mel's Diner Pork Chop Casserole 112

N

Nana's Chicken and Meatball Soup 46
Nana's Fudge Cake 142
Nana's Nuked Chicken And Dumplings 94
Never Fail Dumplings 128
Never Fail Fudge 144
Noodle and Cheese Kugel 131
Noodle Pudding 132
Nuts 33, 35-36, 54, 56, 62, 69-74, 83, 96, 102, 113, 137, 141, 145-146

O

Old Fashioned Pancakes 17
Old Time Beef Stew 91
Orange juice 156
Orange Slush 156
Original Dill Potato Salad 39
Oven Beef Stew 92

P

Pasta 37, 95, 100, 107, 131-132
Pea Lettuce-Onion Salad 37
Pea Soup 47
Peach Cobbler 142
Peach-Berry Punch 154
Peanut Butter Cookies 146
Pear Bread 70
Perfect Potato Pancakes 19
Pie Crust— Flaky 148
Pineapple Lemonade 153
Popovers 23
Pork Chop Dinner 115
Pork Chops—Savory 112
Pot Roast With Dumplings 116

158   Grandma's Favorite Country Recipes

Pot Roast With Golden Potatoes 117
Pot Roast—New England 115
Potato and Leek Soup 44
Potato Bisque Soup 47
Poultry
    Chicken 33, 46, 79, 88, 93-94, 96, 98-104, 117, 120
Prune Bread 69
Pumpkin Bread 70
Pumpkin Muffins—I 71
Pumpkin Muffins—II 72
Pumpkin Pie Filling—Fresh 148
Pumpkin Soup 48

Q
Quiche 25
Quick Raisin Bread 72

R
Raised Buckwheat Pancakes 20
Rice 45, 102-103, 112, 118, 138
Rice Pancakes – Yes, I Said Rice! 21
Rich Man Poor Man Crepes 13
Root Beer—Home Brewed 155

S
Salads 30-31, 33, 35, 37, 39
    Bean and Red Cabbage Salad 32
    Cabbage Slaw 32
    Carrot Salad 33
    Chicken Salad 33
    Fruit Salad Deluxe 35
    German Potato Salad 38
    Hot German Potato Salad 39
    Leftover Turkey Salad 36
    Macaroni 37
    Original Dill Potato Salad 39
    Pea Lettuce Onion Salad 37
    Sicilian Green Bean Salad 36
    Super-Orange-Apricot-Jell-O Salad 40
    Three Bean Salad 31
    Tuna Salad 40
Sangria 155
Sassy Cinnamon Pecan Muffins 73
Sausage-Zucchini Boats 134
Savory Beef Stew 93
Shepherd's Pie 118
Shrimp-Stuffed Acorn Squash 133
Sicilian Green Bean Salad 36
Simple Sweet And Sour Pork 120
Soups 42-43, 45, 47, 49
    Corn Chowder 44
    Cream of Wild Rice Soup 45
    Hobo Soup 49
    Nana's Chicken and Meatball Soup 46
    Pea Soup 47
    Potato and Leek 44
    Potato Bisque Soup 47

Pumpkin 48
Tomato Soup 43
Yellow Squash Soup 50
Zucchini Soup 48
Southern Cornpone 24
Southern Mother's Chicken Fried Steak 97
Spinach Parmesan 136
Spinach Pie 135
Spinach Quiche 27
Squash Muffins 73
Stuffed Cabbage Rolls 118
Stuffed Chicken Breasts 96
Stuffed French Toast 16
Stuffed Mushrooms 81
Stuffed Pork Chops 113
Stuffed Pork Tenderloin 114
Succotash 136
Sunday Quiche 26
Sunday Special Coffee Cake 143
Super-Orange-Apricot-Jell-O Salad 40
Sweet and Sour Meatballs 82-83
Sweet Potato Casserole 137

T
Tequila Chicken 120
Texas Cornbread 74
Tex-Mex Dip 84
The "Best" Oatmeal Cookies 146
The "Other White Meat" Loaf 106
Three Bean Salad 31
Tomato Soup—Fresh 43
Traditional Baked Beans 124
Traditional Cheese Grits 11
Tuna Salad 40

U
Uptown Manhattan Meat Loaf 111

V
Vegetables 122-123, 125, 127, 129, 131, 133, 135, 137
    Artichokes 77
    Asparagus 123
    Avocados 84
    Beans 31-32, 36, 49, 90, 99, 136
    Broccoli 126
    Cabbage 32, 118
    Carrots 33, 43-44, 46-47, 49, 91-94, 101-102, 115, 119, 127
    Cauliflower 126
    Celery 33, 36-39, 43, 45, 47-49, 89, 93, 100, 102, 107, 113, 119, 130
    Corn 12, 44, 74, 99, 127, 136
    Green Beans 129
    Green Peppers 25-26, 31, 36-37, 45, 74, 82, 90, 99, 109, 112, 120, 125, 127
    Mushrooms 22, 26-27, 45, 77, 81, 92, 95, 111, 119, 126, 129, 134-135, 138
    Onions 25-27, 31-33, 36-40, 43-50, 63, 68, 79-84, 88-91, 94-95, 97, 99-103, 107-113, 115-116, 118-120, 125, 127, 130-131, 133-136, 138
    Peas 101
    Potatoes 19, 38-39, 44, 47, 59, 83, 91-92, 99, 115, 117-119, 133
    Pumpkin 48, 62, 70-72, 148
    Red Peppers 103
    Spinach 27, 46, 135-136
    Squash 50, 73, 133
    Sweet Potatoes 137
    Tomatoes 43, 47, 84, 87, 90, 92-93, 99, 107, 112, 125, 134
    Water Chestnuts 119
    Zucchini 21, 48, 74, 77, 108, 126, 134, 144
Vegetables & Sides
Baked Asparagus 123
Baked Hominy 134
Beer Batter Fried Veggies 126
Boston Baked Beans 125
California Baked Beans 125
Carrots Vichy 127
Corn Pudding 127
Country Hominy Grits 128
Easy Potatoes Au Gratin 133
Easy Wild Rice-Mushroom Stuffing 138
Giblet Bread Stuffing 130
Green Bean Casserole 129
Hush Puppies 131
Never Fail Dumplings 128
Noodle and Cheese Kugel 131
Noodle Pudding 132
Sausage-Zucchini Boats 134
Spinach Parmesan 136
Spinach Pie 135
Shrimp-Stuffed Acorn Squash 133
Succotash 136
Sweet Potato Casserole 137
Traditional Baked Beans 124
Vegetable Lasagna 108

W
"Walk The Flank" Steak 105
Wine 119, 155-156
Wine Cooler Punch 156

Y
Yellow Squash Soup 50

Z
Zucchini Cake 144
Zucchini Nut Bread 74
Zucchini Pancakes 21
Zucchini Soup 48

The Artist

Debbie Bell Jarratt, born in Philadelphia, Pennsylvania, began her professional career in art when she joined the design staff at Hallmark Cards in Kansas City, Missouri. She has designed for such companies as Enesco, The Franklin Mint, Goebel, Thomas Nelson Publishers, C.R. Gibson and many more.

Debbie's art appears on millions of products in the form of greeting cards, a variety of collectibles and books.

She now lives in North Carolina with her family. You can see more of Debbie's work on her website, www.debbiebelljarrattgallery.com

The Author

Michael J. Liddy was destined for cooking when at age eight, his grandmother caught him frying baloney in a pan. She affectionately called him "Baloney Bubble" and from then on, he hasn't stopped cooking! From his first job at a modest butcher shop in New Jersey to family restaurants, hospitals, and the famous Arizona Biltmore Hotel, Michael has honed his cooking skills and earned the title "chief cook and bottle washer." Now Michael works for himself in the catering business, which allows him time to test recipes for his cookbooks!

Michael loves cooking and sharing his life with his wife, Dawn, four children, Elizabeth, Alyssa, Dylon, Taylor and new granddaughter, McKenzy. Besides his passion for cooking, Liddy is an excellent musician and tours with "oldies" music artists throughout the country.

If you love Grandma's Favorite Recipes, then you will want more in our Grandma's Favorites Series, chock full of tasty recipes and entertaining Grandma musings. Call, write or visit us online:

602-265-4392/1-800-658-5830
Golden West Publishers
4113 N. Longview Avenue
Phoenix, AZ 85014
www.goldenwestpublishers.com
office@goldenwestpublishers.com